How to Befriend Your Shadow

Welcoming Your Unloved Side

John Monbourquette

How to Befriend Your Shadow

Welcoming Your Unloved Side

NOVALIS

DARTON · LONGMAN + TODD

Cover design: Blair Turner
Cover photograph: Mia & Klaus
Layout: Blaine Herrmann
Translator: Ferdinanda Van Gennip
Editor: Bernadette Gasslein

Business Office:
Novalis
49 Front Street East, 2nd Floor
Toronto, Ontario, Canada
M5E 1B3

Phone: 1-800-387-7164 or (416) 363-3303
Fax: 1-800-204-4140 or (416) 363-9409
E-mail: novalis@interlog.com

First published in French in 1997 by Novalis, Bayard-Éditions and Les Éditions du Centurion.

English translation published in 2001 by Novalis, Saint Paul University, Ottawa, Canada and Darton, Longman and Todd Ltd, 1 Spencer Court, 140-142 Wandsworth High Street, London SW18 4JJ U.K.

We acknowledge the financial support of the Government of Canada through the Book Publishing Industry Development Program (BPIDP) for our publishing activities.

Canadian Cataloguing in Publication Data

Monbourquette, Jean
How to befriend your shadow: Welcoming your unloved side

Translation of: Apprivoiser son ombre.
Includes bibliographical references.
ISBN 2-89507-082-2

1. Shadow (Psychoanalysis) 2. Self-actualization
(Psychology) 3. Self-presentation. 4. Self-knowledge, Theory of.
5. Persona (Psychanalysis) 6. Spritual life. I. Title.

BF175.5.S55M6613 2001 155.2 C00-901702-X

A catalogue record for this book is available from the British Library.
ISBN 0-232-52430-0

Printed in Canada.

About the author

John Monbourquette is a psychotherapist, bestselling author and Roman Catholic priest. While he has both taught high school and worked as a parish priest, his principal interest has been in the relationship between spirituality and psychology. His graduate studies in theology and psychology, and his doctoral studies in psychology at the International College of Los Angeles, have enabled him to pursue these interests both in the academic world, where he was for many years a professor in the Pastoral Institute of Saint Paul University, Ottawa, and in his own private practice as a psychologist. His special areas of interest include forgiveness, self-esteem, male violence, the dynamics of grief, and accompanying the dying.

He has given hundreds of conferences on these topics in Canada and Europe to both professional and lay audiences. He is the author (under his French name, Jean Monbourquette) of eight books in French. Three of these (*To Love Again* – reissued in 2001 as *How to Love Again: Moving from Grief to Growth* – which has sold over 175,000 copies in six languages around the world; *Growing Through Loss: A Handbook for Grief Support Groups;* and *How to Forgive: A Step-by-Step Guide*) are available in English; a fourth, on the subject of finding your mission, will be published in Fall 2001. Monbourquette is co-author of three other books and has written many articles for professional journals.

TABLE OF CONTENTS

Introduction 8

Chapter 1:
The Shadow – An Unexplored and Untapped Treasury
• Loving the Enemy Within Me 10
• What is the shadow? 11
• Healthy personal growth needs shadow work. 13
• For healthy social relationships, befriend your shadow. 15
• Shadow reintegration work and the development of moral life . . 17
• To grow spiritually, reintegrate the shadow 20

Chapter 2:
The Jungian Concept of the Shadow
• Carl Jung's Dream About His Shadow. 24
• Through theory to self-understanding 25
• Jung's search for a theory of the shadow 25
• The shadow: a metaphor to describe repressed material. 28
• The various forms of the shadow 29
• How to classify the shadow 30

Chapter 3:
The Formation of the Shadow
• The Story of the Man with the Seven Masks 36
• The formation of the persona 37
• Persona and false self. 41
• Formation of a virulent and dissociated shadow 42

Chapter 4:
Welcoming Your Shadow
• The Wolf of Gubbio 52
• Three ways of understanding the unconscious:
Freud, Nietzsche, Jung 53
• Three pitfalls to avoid in shadow work 55
• How to manage your encroaching shadow 60

Chapter 5:
Recognizing Your Shadow
• The Story of the Lost Wallet.......... 72
• Looking in the right place.......... 73
• Denying the existence of your shadow.......... 73
• Strategies for recognizing your shadow.......... 74
• How to recognize someone else's shadow.......... 85

Chapter 6:
Owning Your Projections Again
• The Story of the Woodcutter Who Had Lost His Axe.......... 88
• The influence of shadow projections.......... 89
• What does it mean to project your shadow onto someone else?.......... 90
• "Re-appropriating" shadow projections.......... 97
• Jesus Christ denounces unhealthy projection.......... 103

Chapter 7:
Strategies for Befriending Your Shadow
• Loading My New Boat.......... 106
• How strategies work.......... 107
• Conditions for reintegrating your shadow and your conscious self.......... 108
• Strategies for befriending your shadow.......... 110

Chapter 8:
Reintegration of the Shadow and Spiritual Development
• The Story of the Spring of Living Water.......... 126
• The shadow and morality.......... 127
• The shadow and the spiritual life.......... 130

Notes.......... 149
Bibliography.......... 153

There is untold wealth to be tapped from the notion of the shadow. My interest in this question began in the 1970s, when I studied the analytical psychology of Carl Jung. Later this interest was rekindled at a workshop called "Eating Your Shadow," given by the American poet and thinker Robert Bly. Since then, my fascination with this subject has only increased. I saw the benefits of exploring the concept of the shadow for both my own personal growth and that of my clients.

My lectures and workshops on the theme of the shadow have allowed me to share my enthusiasm for the usefulness of this notion with a wide audience. This book was inspired by the response from my audiences, and combines the results of my research and my own reflections.

Is our shadow a friend or an enemy? That will depend entirely on how we view it and interact with it. At first it will appear to be an enemy. But gradually we can welcome and befriend it. That is the challenge this book holds out to you, the challenge of welcoming and befriending your shadow.

Each chapter begins with a story to let you, the reader, get an intuitive grasp of the ideas to be developed in that chapter. Wherever possible, examples from real life support theoretical considerations. The exercises in Chapters 5 and 6 invite you to take an active part in your own personal growth.

I wish to thank two people in particular for their support in the preparation of this book. Jacques Croteau, my colleague and friend, once again generously assisted by improving the style and critiquing certain points. His meticulous revision and persistence in clarifying ambiguities contributed significantly to the quality of the writing.

Journalist Pauline Vertefeuille played the part of the general reader. Her spontaneous reactions and judicious comments on the organization of certain sections helped improve the clarity of the text.

LOVING THE ENEMY WITHIN ME

One Sabbath day, the son of a rabbi went to pray at another rabbi's synagogue. On his return, his father asked him, "Well, did you learn anything new?" The son replied, "I certainly did!" His rabbinical pride somewhat hurt, the father continued nevertheless, "So, what do they teach over there?" "Love your enemy!" came the answer. The father exclaimed eagerly, "Why, they preach the same thing as I do. How can you say you learned something new?" His son explained, "They taught me to love the enemy that lives within me, the one I am so desperately trying to fight."

The Shadow: An Unexplored and Untapped Treasury

It is not by looking into the light that we become luminous, but by plunging into the darkness. However, this is often unpleasant work, and therefore not very popular.

– Carl G. Jung

WHAT IS THE SHADOW?

Consider this book my invitation to you to embark on a great adventure: to get acquainted with your shadow. The shadow side of the personality is a mysterious reality that intrigues and sometimes frightens us. Is it friend or foe? This depends on how we view it and how we interact with it.

Exactly what is the shadow? The answer to this question will become clear as you work your way through the chapters of this book. However, here at the outset I will try to shed a little light on this evanescent dimension of our being. The shadow is everything we have driven back into the unconscious for fear of being rejected by people who played a determining role in our upbringing. We were afraid we would lose their affection if we disappointed them or made them uncomfortable through certain behaviours or aspects of our personality. We soon learned to discern what was acceptable in their eyes and what was not. So, to please them, we eagerly relegated large portions of ourselves to the faraway realms of the unconscious. We did our utmost to avoid the slightest verbal or tacit disapproval from those we loved and on whom we depended.

Keen to be appreciated by others, we showed ourselves to be kind and polite. To do this, we had to repress everything that might appear deviant, shameful or reprehensible. Needing to be appreciated, we conformed to the requirements, rules and

Gradually, a whole underground world was constructed deep inside us, made up of repressed and suppressed material accumulated over the years.

regulations of our milieu. We strove to camouflage anything that seemed to displease or shock those around us.

We took into account that, in certain environments, being ready to help others was viewed favourably, while thinking of ourselves was considered selfish. Obedience was valued, but assertiveness certainly was not. Being nice was acceptable, but getting angry would upset people. Hiding any sexual feelings was well received but expressing them even slightly was frowned upon.

Gradually, a whole underground world was constructed deep inside us, made up of repressed and suppressed material accumulated over the years. Finally, we were left sitting on a sort of psychic volcano that threatened to erupt at any time. This psychic energy, compressed but still very much alive and active, is what we call the shadow. The shadow is "this dark treasury [that] includes our infantile parts, emotional attachments, neurotic symptoms, as well as our undeveloped talents and gifts. The shadow … retains contact with the lost depths of the soul, with life and vitality … even the creative…."[1]

Far from being sterile and inactive, this wild and undeveloped entity of our being constantly demands that we acknowledge and tap into it. Woe to those who continue to ignore it! Like a raging torrent, it will one day force its way into the conscious and invade it. On the other hand, if we welcome the shadow warmly, we will be able to befriend it. In turn, it will reveal the rich resources it can offer us. The work of befriending our shadow, then, consists of this: reintegrating into the zone of the conscious these eclipsed aspects of ourselves and reclaiming them so that, as persons, we may blossom as fully as possible.

I would like to stress the fundamental importance of working on the reintegration of the shadow, for the sake of our psychological and social development as well as for our moral and spiritual growth.

Making peace with our shadow and befriending it are fundamental to authentic self-esteem.

HEALTHY PERSONAL GROWTH NEEDS SHADOW WORK

The shadow and self-knowledge

Unless you know your shadow, you can't really know yourself! Doing personal work on the shadow is essential for anyone who wants to become a balanced and whole person. Acknowledging and reintegrating our shadow lets us recover parts of ourselves that we repressed for fear of social rejection. As we are growing up, we can be ashamed or afraid of certain feelings or emotions, qualities, talents or aptitudes, interests, ideas or attitudes, because they are poorly received by those around us. This makes us tend to repress them and consign them to the labyrinths of the unconscious. Now, these unloved aspects of ourselves remain very much alive and try to assert themselves, even after we have repressed them. If we do not own them, they will work against us, making us fearful and causing serious psychological and social problems.

Threatening as it may seem, bringing to light these untapped resources of our being allows us to appropriate and reintegrate them. Thus will be fulfilled the basic condition for all human growth, "Know thyself" – the famous precept inscribed at the portal of the temple at Delphi.

The shadow and self-esteem

Making peace with our shadow and befriending it are fundamental to authentic self-esteem. How can we love ourselves or have confidence in ourselves if part of us, our shadow side, is ignored and works against our own interests? I was astonished to find that current writing on self-esteem is not

No one can afford to dispense with the work of reintegrating the shadow.

more concerned with the disastrous consequences of leaving the shadow in its wild state, where it becomes a major source of low self-esteem and low regard for others.

Carl Jung reminds us that the human psyche is the stage where many intimate battles take place. He reminds us that the strangest and most moving dramas are not the ones acted out in the theatre but those that take place in the hearts of ordinary men and women. Their lives do not attract special attention. Nor do they betray any sign of the conflicts raging inside them – unless they fall victim to a depression, the cause of which they themselves are unaware.[2]

Therefore, no one can afford to dispense with the work of reintegrating the shadow. If we refuse to do this work on ourselves, we risk psychological imbalance. We will tend to feel tense and depressed, tormented by vague feelings of anxiety, self-dissatisfaction and guilt; we will fall victim to all sorts of obsessions and be easily carried away by our impulses: jealousy, uncontrolled anger, resentment, inappropriate sexual behaviour, greediness, and so forth.

Let's take a look at alcoholism and drug addiction, two of the most common addictions that wreak such havoc in our societies today. Sam Naifeh, in an excellent article on the causes of addiction, states, "Addiction is a shadow problem."[3] In fact, the compulsive attraction to alcohol and drugs represents a poorly-chosen means to get in touch with the shadow side of our being. Much as we try to blame toxic substances for human degeneration, they are merely an indirect cause in that they allow their users to access the unconscious. They make it possible for addicts to identify briefly with the dark side of the self, which is a constant source of obsession. The alcoholic's sober self remains constantly dissatisfied as long as the alcoholic self has not been recovered from its hiding place in the shadow.

The shadow and creativity

Author Julien Green, referring to the life of his shadow, observed, "Someone whom I do not know, but whom I would like to know, writes my books." The patient and intelligent work of befriending your shadow will reveal immense potential that has remained buried, undeveloped, in your unconscious. Actualizing this potential will produce a surplus of vitality and stimulate creativity in all the dimensions of your life.

People grappling with a projection of their shadow have a disturbed perception of reality.

FOR HEALTHY SOCIAL RELATIONSHIPS, BEFRIEND YOUR SHADOW

Shadow projection causes disturbed perception

If we do not acknowledge and welcome our shadow, it will not only create obsessions but also force its way into the conscious in the form of projections onto others. Let me say a few words now about the phenomenon of shadow projection, which I will develop more fully in Chapter 6.

How does shadow projection affect the social environment? People grappling with a projection of their shadow have a disturbed perception of reality. They attribute to others the traits or qualities that they refused to recognize in themselves, thus imposing a mask on others. They tend to idealize, look down on or be afraid of those wearing their projections. In short, the "projector" (the one doing the projecting) ends up being afraid of the projections of their own shadow. They see their shadow reflected in others who, like mirrors reflecting distorted images, then become fascinating or threatening. In the chapter devoted to shadow projection, we will examine the effects of this phenomenon on passionate love as well as on workplace relationships.

When this phenomenon occurs in social relationships, expect conflicts. By a curious reversal, the shadow's projections

If people project their own weaknesses or shortcomings onto another person, how can they possibly tolerate, let alone love, that other person?

reflect back onto the "projector" who, haunted by them, becomes their victim and is fascinated or repulsed by them. Like the boxer who trains by fighting his own shadow, the shadow "projector" is condemned to this exhausting, never-ending exercise of shadow boxing.

Resolving the conflicts created by projected shadows

If people project their own weaknesses or shortcomings onto another person, how can they possibly tolerate, let alone love, that other person, whether it be their boss, neighbour, spouse or child? The person on whom the shadow is projected will get on their nerves; the "projector" will be obsessed with them. Here we are touching on the root cause of most interpersonal conflicts and of professional burnout, topics we will deal with in the next few chapters.

Clearly it is a precious asset for mediators involved in the resolution of interpersonal conflict to be familiar with the games, reflections and effects of the shadow. Such knowledge enables them, first of all, to detect reciprocal shadow projections between the antagonists, and then to help them re-appropriate their respective shadows. No other classic problem-solving technique has proven to be effective in resolving this type of conflict. In fact, the confusion created by the mutual projections of the two adversaries cannot be disentangled in any other way.

This is why more and more professors of human relations are teaching shadow theory: to inform participants of the perverse effect of such projections. For example, business managers and supervisors are being trained to be aware of their shadow and the effects of projecting it onto their employees. In this way, managers can avoid becoming sources of conflict within their own organizations.[4]

Likewise, to facilitate the smooth operation of a business, some human relations counsellors focus on helping to reveal the shadow of the organization itself, so that the factors causing disruption can be brought to light.[5]

To facilitate the smooth operation of a business, some human relations counsellors focus on helping to reveal the shadow of the organization itself.

Note, by the way, that marriage counsellors continually grapple with this type of conflict, which arises from the mutual projections of the spouses.

Carl Jung believed that becoming aware of our projections onto others and then being able to take back what we have projected not only produces improved interpersonal relations, but also has a beneficial effect on society as a whole. He believed that making the effort to get along with our shadow to the point of reintegrating our projections constitutes an act that is useful to the whole world. Jung said that no matter how small such an act might seem, it represents a contribution to solving the enormous and insurmountable problems of our times.[6]

SHADOW REINTEGRATION WORK AND THE DEVELOPMENT OF MORAL LIFE

From a legalistic morality to a conscience-based morality

The psychological work of reintegrating our shadow directly influences the formation of moral conscience and plays an indispensable role in it. Carl Jung went so far as to say, "The shadow is a moral problem that challenges the whole ego-personality, for no one can become conscious of the shadow without considerable moral effort. To become conscious of it involves recognizing the dark aspects of the personality as present and real."[7]

In *Depth Psychology and a New Ethic,* Eric Neumann, one of Jung's great disciples, focuses on showing the importance of

The moral codes of a culture determine what is permitted and what is forbidden.

psychological work in the formation of moral conscience. Our moral conscience begins mainly as simple obedience to the rules and moral codes transmitted by the family and by the community. Admirable as that may be, we must seek to go beyond this first stage, for moral imperatives of a family or a society promote certain behaviours and discourage others. Compare, for example, the values held sacred in a Native American society with those held sacred in a capitalist society. Native Americans favour community values over individual values, while our capitalist societies strongly favour the spirit of the individual over the spirit of the community.

The moral codes of a culture determine what is permitted and what is forbidden. To conform to them, we are led to repress certain moral qualities that our milieu considers to be of little importance or perhaps unacceptable. If we do not free ourselves from some of the conditioning imposed on us by a given culture, there is a grave risk that we will leave untapped an entire set of values neglected by the environment in which we were raised. For this reason, an ethic based on a notion as arbitrary and incomplete as that of good and evil can only hamper the formation of a true moral conscience. Think, for example, of the *lex talionis,* whose harmful consequences were pointed out by Gandhi: "If you follow the old justice code – an eye for an eye and a tooth for a tooth – you will create a blind and toothless world," he said.

Behaviour based on narrow moral vision results in a corresponding shadow. This shadow will seek to express itself through obsessions and scruples and, at other times, will be projected onto others in the form of rigid moral prejudices, as we shall see below.

Legalistic morality and the "scapegoat mentality"

Instead of projecting onto others the disordered tendencies of their shadow, the new moral person recognizes that these lie within.

Eric Neumann considers an ethic that is concerned solely with determining what is good and what is evil to be deficient, as it does not help the person discover in themselves the root of the evil and find the means to destroy it. In contrast to this ethic, which he calls "The Old Ethic," Neumann proposes a new one – "The New Ethic." Here the essence of forming moral conscience consists first and foremost of the work of reintegrating our shadow. He sees this psychospiritual work as a determining element for a true moral conscience. Instead of projecting onto others the disordered tendencies of their shadow, the new moral person recognizes that these lie within, assumes responsibility for them and then reintegrates them into a coherent moral life.

The Old Ethic eventually leads to the creation of a scapegoat mentality. It begins by manifesting itself in someone's personal life as a source of relational hostilities and conflicts. When transposed onto a national scale, this mentality risks taking on gigantic proportions. At that level, the shadow tends to vilify neighbouring nations and mandate itself to destroy them. This has been the source of numerous armed conflicts in history. Following the same logic, foreigners, minorities and people who are "different" are more likely to be the target of projections and, eventually, to become scapegoats. Neumann believes that only a new ethic will enable nations to recognize their own perverse tendencies instead of projecting them. Perhaps we need to recall at this point that the projections of the collective shadow are not innocuous, but can engender persecution and slaughter, as was all too clearly proven by the Nazi extermination of the Jews.

Two periods in the human life cycle are particularly vulnerable to shadow development: the beginning of the spiritual life and mid-life.

TO GROW SPIRITUALLY, REINTEGRATE THE SHADOW

More than ever before, we urgently need to find a healthy and solid psychology of the soul, capable of fostering the development of an authentic spiritual life. The analytical psychology developed by Jung, who was a very spiritual person, can make a contribution here. In fact, it provides the means for the "discernment of spirits," which is not unrelated to the discernment of the shadow and the "spirits" that inhabit it. It is because they failed to practise this discernment that numerous professionals of the spiritual life behaved in ways that are both morally and spiritually unacceptable. We have only to think of the deviant behaviours that have been exposed recently in priests, pastors, spiritual directors and the founders of sects.

Two periods in the human life cycle are particularly vulnerable to shadow development: the beginning of the spiritual life and mid-life. These periods have "an initiatory value and significance for someone's construction of personal and social identity, for their way of fitting into society and also for defining certain relationships with others."[8] In the final chapter of this book, we will examine in greater depth the connection between the reintegration of the shadow and the spiritual life. However, I would like to say a few words here about these two important periods.

The spiritual life of the novice

One day some disciples asked their master what path they should follow in order to have a solid start in the spiritual life. He answered them, "Learn first to overcome your fears." What words of great wisdom! Indeed, the novice's first task is to examine their weaknesses, fears, revulsions and antipathies. Carl Jung's advice was: "Find out what a person is most afraid of and you will know what their next stage of growth will be."

Without deep and honest self-acceptance, the spiritual life rests on a dangerous psychological foundation and is nothing more than escape into a world of illusion. Humble self-knowledge is the most basic condition for any true spirituality.

Without deep and honest self-acceptance, the spiritual life rests on a dangerous psychological foundation.

The spiritual life in middle age

To describe the situation of those who have reached mid-life, anthropologist and mythologist Joseph Campbell uses this metaphor: "We spend the first thirty-five or forty years of our existence climbing a tall ladder in order to finally reach the top of a building; then, once we're on the roof, we realize it's the wrong building."

At this stage it is natural to take stock of what we have achieved. We believe we're someone because we've made our mark in society. We review what we have accomplished and what we have let go of, our joys and our sorrows, our successes and our failures, our realized hopes and our unfulfilled dreams. Only rarely are we fully satisfied with what we see. We always observe in our lives some rather serious deficiencies. The spectre of death becomes more real. In response, some people focus on rejuvenation. Others switch careers or end their marriage. There are those who start a new lifestyle. In other words, in middle age, many people would like to start all over again.

At that point they need to ask themselves, "Should I be satisfied with changing just how my life looks on the

The challenge of this period is to explore the world of possibilities lying fallow within us.

outside? Don't I first need to delve deep inside?" The answer is clear. After we have devoted so many years of our lives to building a strong ego and becoming a contributing member of society, the challenge of this period is to explore the world of possibilities lying fallow within us. The crisis of mid-life demands that we tap the potential buried in the shadow. Not to do so is to jeopardize our full spiritual development.

Don't expect that getting in touch with your shadow and tapping into its riches will be smooth sailing. But it is a wonderful experience for anyone who is willing to work on welcoming home the shadow. This book is offered as a guide for those who feel drawn to embark on the adventure of full self-realization.

CARL JUNG'S DREAM ABOUT HIS SHADOW

I had a dream which both frightened and encouraged me. It was night in some unknown place, and I was making slow and painful headway against a mighty wind. Dense fog was flying along everywhere. I had my hands cupped around a tiny light which threatened to go out at any moment. Everything depended on my keeping this little light alive. Suddenly I had the feeling that something was coming up behind me. I looked back, and saw a gigantic black figure following me. But at the same moment I was conscious, in spite of my terror, that I must keep my little light going through night and wind, regardless of all dangers. When I awoke I realized at once that the figure was my own shadow on the swirling mists, brought into being by the little light I was carrying. I knew, too, that this little light was my consciousness, the only light I have. Though infinitely small and fragile in comparison with the powers of darkness, it is still a light, my only light.[9]

The Jungian Concept of the Shadow

Forget your profile;
it is out of fashion.
But pay attention to the one
walking close to you
whose existence you do not believe in.

– Antonio Machado

THROUGH THEORY TO SELF-UNDERSTANDING

The shadow does not reveal itself easily. A Jungian psychologist claimed that a person who had no idea of the shadow and its effects would not be able to guess that it existed. This shows how important it is for us to have a theoretical understanding of the shadow if we are eventually to experience it.

In my view, the school of analytical psychology of Carl Gustav Jung and his followers offers the clearest and most practical theory of the shadow. This theory places the shadow in the context of human development as a whole, thus providing the means to get in touch with it. My comments on the shadow have, to a large extent, been inspired by this theory.

JUNG'S SEARCH FOR A THEORY OF THE SHADOW

Jung, being familiar with Freudian psychoanalysis, was aware of the repressed world of the unconscious. But the idea that it was formed by the repression of personal psychological

For Jung, the shadow represented a set of complexes, of repressed energies.

entities did not satisfy him. He needed to go further. His research into myths, dreams and psychotic disillusionment, as well as his study of drawings by children and "primitive" people, led him to conclude that there was another deeper unconscious, what he called the "collective unconscious." He conceived of this as a memory of a set of images or themes, innate in and common to all of humanity. To these universal configurations he gave the name "archetypes," as they can be found in all civilizations. In his view, the shadow appeared to be one of these fundamental archetypes. This major discovery by Jung ended his long friendship with Freud who, from then on, considered his disciple a heretic with respect to the beliefs held by the Freudian school.

For Jung, the shadow represented a set of complexes, of repressed energies, which Freud had called the "Id." Through all the ages, the shadow, as Jung understood it, had appeared in myths and stories in the form of various archetypes: the "dark brother," the "double," the "twins" (where one of them demonstrates a sinister character), the "alter ego," and so forth. At first Jung thought of this shadow as abstract and anonymous but, gradually, as he studied his own dreams and those of his patients, it became a concrete, personal image. As early as 1912, Jung was speaking of the "shadow side of the psyche." Later, he would use various expressions to designate the shadow, such as "the repressed self," "the alter ego," "the dark side of the self," "the alienated self," "one's inferior personality."

In 1917, in his work *On the Psychology of the Unconscious*, he describes the shadow as "the other in us," "the unconscious personality [in us] of the other sex," "the loathsome inferior [in us]," or "the other [in us] who embarrasses and shames us." He defines it as "the negative side of the personality, the sum total of all the disagreeable qualities we tend to hate and to conceal, as well as our underdeveloped functions and the content of the personal unconscious."[10] However, we should add that while the shadow may appear incompatible with the ideas and values passed on in a given milieu, it is not intrinsically something bad.

The following diagram illustrates Jung's concept of the psyche.

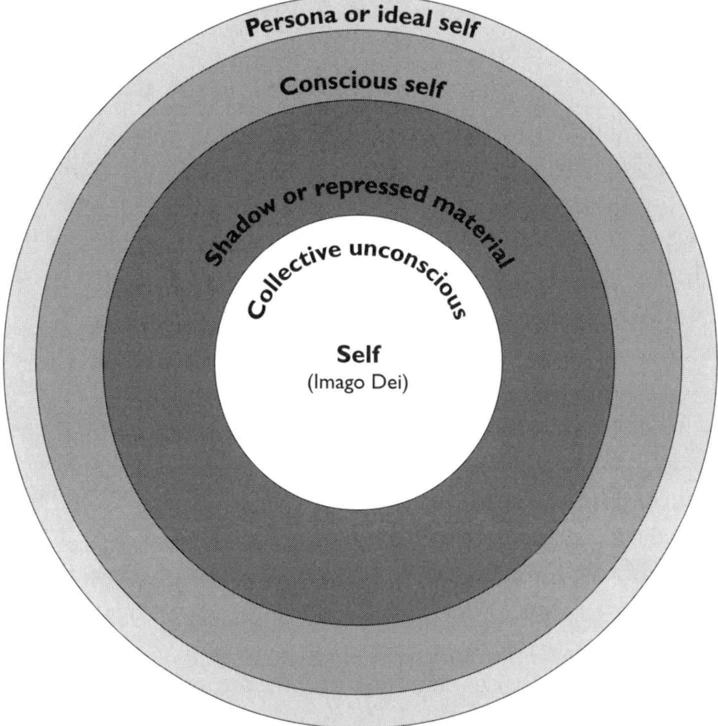

The self: the centre of the psyche; unconscious and conscious
The self (ego): the conscious part of the psyche
The persona: the part that adapts to one's milieu
The shadow: the part that is repressed through the desire to adapt

If the ego is a person's conscious place, the shadow is its unconscious flipside.

THE SHADOW: A METAPHOR TO DESCRIBE REPRESSED MATERIAL

The image evoked by the term "shadow," as first used by Jung and later taken up by his followers, represents well all the repressed material of the unconscious organized into a counterpart to what the conscious ego lives. A person's shadow is thus that psychic material crystallized in the unconscious to compensate for the one-dimensional development of the conscious self. Like a light, the conscious self produces an unconscious dark area: the shadow. In short, if the ego is a person's conscious place, the shadow is its unconscious flipside.

The shadow is a good image to illustrate the repressed world. Normally, we like to be guided by light when we walk. When the light is ahead of us, we are unable to see the shadow that follows us; others often notice it before we do. Similarly, others often see more clearly than we do the dark side of our personality that we refuse to acknowledge.

The shadow, which is quite short under the midday sun, grows taller, its length increasing in proportion to the fading of daylight. Then, throughout the night, it fills all space. This is what happens with our psychic shadow. A minuscule presence during our waking hours, it becomes an enormous presence during our sleep, where it edges its way into our dreams.

Thus, everything we tried to hide during the day to save face is revealed to us at night by our dreams. It is as if our dreams want to re-establish the portion of truth that we have covered up. So, the repulsive and threatening symbols that sometimes make up the fabric of our dreams can be a real surprise to us. They brutally expose repressed material: a mother will take on the appearance of a witch; a boss, that of a tyrant; a neighbour, that of a prostitute; and so forth. Dreams shed a harsh light on what's behind those white lies we tell so easily to keep up appearances and conform to the rules of proper etiquette. Reportedly, certain Buddhist monks, who are no longer concerned with saving face in society, no longer dream. Owing to their self-deprecating humour, they almost never harbour ulterior motives anymore.

The shadow can take on one of two forms: the black shadow or the white shadow.

Expressions using the image of the shadow illustrate effectively the kinds of reactions that the repressed psychic world provokes in us. For instance, we say that people who are plagued by fear and anxiety are "afraid of their own shadow." Or when someone has fallen under the spell of another person, we say they "follow them around like their shadow." Sending a detective out to catch someone in the act of a crime is called "putting a shadow on someone." Then there is the German proverb: "You can't jump over your own shadow." In other words, you cannot run away from your repressed psychic world.

THE VARIOUS FORMS OF THE SHADOW

The dark shadow and the white shadow

Depending on the nature of the repressed material, the shadow can take on one of two forms: the black shadow or the white shadow. The black shadow results from the repression of instincts such as sexuality and aggressivity. It manifests itself particularly in those who have acquired a reputation for being upright and virtuous. Sometimes the black shadow they have wanted to deny rises up against the values of their milieu, causing them to revolt against the rules of society, break the law, compete with others, be envious and jealous, want to dominate or give in to unrestrained sexual impulses.

The white shadow, however, results from the lack of development or repression of any virtuous or spiritual inclination.

The white shadow, however, results from the lack of development or repression of any virtuous or spiritual inclination. It originates in family and social pressure exerted on an individual from a very young age, imposing deviant attitudes and behaviours as the norm. Here are four examples of white shadow. A "mafioso," whose sole ambition in life is to exploit people, represses his natural tendencies to honesty or generosity. His white shadow is therefore composed of the repressed virtues of honesty and compassion. In another case, a juvenile delinquent gained popularity with his gang for his unruly behaviour and school pranks. He became convinced that observing the law was bad; therefore he should suppress any urge towards discipline in his life. To adhere to discipline thus became part of his white shadow. In the third example, a man living a loose lifestyle finds sexually disciplined behaviour totally repulsive to him. He had buried the natural virtue of chastity in his shadow. The last example involves a militant atheist who, when drunk, exhibits the strange behaviour of kneeling down to pray. His drunken state allows him to set free his spiritual side. The world of the spiritual life forms the white side of his shadow.

HOW TO CLASSIFY THE SHADOW

A shadow is classified differently according to the environment that has produced it. It can be a family shadow, an institutional shadow or a national shadow.

The family shadow

Families convey not only positive values and convictions, but also shadow zones resulting from collective repression. Thus, tragic events that have befallen a family may be transformed into myths. Similarly, if a death in the family was not handled well, it may continue to haunt them; family scandals may become well-guarded secrets. Moreover, when wounds, tragedies and dramas remain on the unconscious level of the family memory, they tend to reproduce themselves in each successive generation. From a single event, the descendants of each generation are led to re-live the same dramas and to repress the same things without knowing exactly why.

The descendants of each generation are led to re-live the same dramas and to repress the same things without knowing exactly why.

I can think of a family where the parents forbade their children to go swimming. They insisted on this rule as an absolute, although they could not explain why. However, those who knew the family's history could guess the unconscious motive for the taboo: their great-grandparents had lost two sons through a drowning accident, and all their descendants since had an irrational fear of water.

This is not an isolated case. In all families, both to avoid uncomfortable situations and out of a subconscious sense of family loyalty, parents semi-consciously forbid their children to express certain emotions or develop particular qualities or talents so that they adopt a specific way of behaving. By doing this, parents are obeying the impulses of the family shadow. These expectations carry the force of law in the family. Children, being fearful of and sensitive to the least risk of rejection, readily comply with these parental rules. This mechanism is all the more effective as non-verbal prohibitions enter the unconscious more easily and thus have greater persuasive power.

Professionals who subscribe to the theory of Transactional Analysis have inventoried some of these family prohibitions and found that they are all formulated negatively. Here is a brief list: don't exist; don't be yourself; don't be a boy (a girl); don't be a child; don't grow up; don't succeed; don't be healthy; don't get involved or don't get intimate in your

Sometimes the shadow of an entire family is concentrated on just one of its members.

relationships; don't think; don't feel. It would no doubt be of interest to describe how such messages influence the development of the shadow in the child. However, such a description would take us beyond the immediate purpose of this book.

Sometimes the shadow of an entire family is concentrated on just one of its members. It is the classic case of the "black sheep" who deviates from the family rules and norms. The "identified patient," as current family therapy terms him or her, has the role of ensuring balance in a deficient family system. The therapist's delicate task consists then of helping the family to recognize that it is the entire family system that is defective, not just the "black sheep," who merely reflects the family's dysfunction. Through his or her behaviour, this one individual reveals the deficient aspect of the entire family's growth. For example, frivolousness or irresponsibility on the part of an "identified patient" will bring to light the side of a family that is too rigid and serious.

The institutional shadow

Human communities are inclined to favour certain values over others that they consider useless and even wrong. A community founder's shadow, along with the corresponding taboos and restrictions, leaves its imprint on the shadow of the group. Even after he or she has died, the founder's spirit and shadow will haunt the members of the community.

The following case illustrates the creation of an institutional shadow. Two directors of a house of priestly formation became extremely preoccupied with detecting the slightest signs of either homosexuality or alcoholism among the seminarians. The innocent gesture of tapping a friend on the shoulder was interpreted as a sign of homosexuality.

Gulping down an alcoholic drink was seen to indicate the lack of self-control associated with the alcoholic. As a result, every member of this institution became obsessed with ferreting out homosexuality and alcoholism. Seminarians began to spy on one another, looking for possible signs of these "faults." The shadows of the two directors involved had finally poisoned the minds of everyone around them. Diligence in study and prayer, kindness, camaraderie, healthy human relations – all values that deserved to be encouraged – received little attention from the directors and seminarians. They remained fixated on tracking down homosexuality and alcoholism.

An institution that cannot recognize its shadow will gradually begin to deviate from its goals. But, worse still, completely fascinated by its shadow, it will end up promoting the very thing it is trying to avoid.

The national shadow

Shadows also exist on a national scale.

Shadows also exist on a national scale. To become aware of this, simply visit a foreign country. We notice very quickly that the people of this country think differently from our fellow citizens. A shortcoming in our own country will perhaps be considered a quality in another. For example, an American's direct yes or no in response to a question may seem to lack sensitivity to a Canadian, while the latter's reliance on body language and tone rather than directness in words may well be considered dishonest or weak by an American.

The more a nation isolates itself, the more it becomes blind to its faults and failings, and the more it will tend to project its fears, loathings and old stereotypes on its neighbours. Only assiduous contact between different

Until people have learned to know and appreciate foreign customs, they will feed the prejudice created by their own national shadow.

peoples makes it possible to recognize the shortcomings and faults of their national character. Until people have learned to know and appreciate foreign customs, they will feed the prejudice created by their own national shadow. Racist nicknames and jokes that target neighbouring peoples are sure signs of national shadow projection.

During wartime, the media support and reinforce the projection of the collective shadow onto "the enemy." Everything we consider hateful and reprehensible in ourselves we try desperately to identify with our adversary. During World War II, the Germans had every fault imaginable. During the Cold War that followed, it was the Russians' turn to be maligned. For a long time African-Americans have been the target of shadow projection by those of European ancestry. Jews likewise have been the chosen victims of the collective shadow of several other peoples. Difference and originality, whether found in minorities, in foreigners or in great minds, always disturb. And so we expose them so we can turn them into scapegoats who bear all the evil tendencies in the national shadow.

Are whole nations thus condemned forever to creating enemies or scapegoats and saddling them with their collective shadow? Or are we allowed to dream that one day all nations will look at one another in all truth and that each will befriend their own shadow instead of projecting it onto another nation and seeking to destroy it?

So-called primitive societies instinctively found a way to correct the deviations of their collective shadow: certain members of their community were designated to "play" the collective shadow, thus allowing the group to relativize their customs and ways of thinking. Among the American Sioux, it was the Heyhoka who exercised this sacred ministry of representing the group's shadow. Systematically, he would perform a series of activities backwards: he would mount a horse facing its hindquarters; he would construct his tent with its opening facing in the opposite direction of that of the other tents; he would even defecate during religious ceremonies.[11] He would constantly take pleasure in violating the rules and norms of the tribe.

Today, political satirists and comedians mirror back to us our national shadow, exposing our common shortcomings.

The jester or fool in the king's court played a similar role for the sovereign: the fool would reveal to the king all that his court tried to hide from him.

Finally, consider what the "fools' feast" during the Middle Ages was designed to reveal. On that day, social positions were reversed: the "village idiot" was crowned king; donkeys were made to "celebrate Mass" in place of prelates. Today, political satirists and comedians partially fulfill this function. They mirror back to us our national shadow, exposing our common shortcomings.

Ever since Jung's first intuitions about the existence and nature of the shadow, we have witnessed a proliferation of writing on the subject. Jung might agree with his followers on all points. We know, in fact, how much he feared that they would quote him as saying things he never thought and develop theories that contradicted his thinking. One day, when he was asked to clarify more precisely his understanding of the shadow, he refused, simply repeating whimsically, "The shadow is everything in our unconscious." I hope that my efforts to clarify Jung's understanding of the shadow in order to help you in your psychological and spiritual growth have not distorted Jung's thought.

THE MAN WITH THE SEVEN MASKS

Once upon a time there was a man who wore seven different masks, one for each day of the week. When he got up in the morning, he covered his face immediately with one of the masks. Then he got dressed and left for work. He lived this way without ever showing his true face.

Now, one night while he was asleep, a thief stole his seven masks. As soon as he woke up and realized what had happened, he began to scream at the top of his lungs, "Help! I've been robbed!" Then he set out scouring every street in the town in search of his masks. The people saw him gesticulating and swearing and threatening the whole world with the worst disasters if he didn't recover his masks. He spent the entire day looking for the robber, but to no avail. Desperate and inconsolable, he broke down, crying like a child. The people tried to comfort him, but nothing could console him.

A woman passing by stopped and asked him, "What's the matter, my friend? Why are you crying so?" He looked up and answered, choking back his tears, "They stole my masks and, with my face exposed like this, I feel too vulnerable." "Take comfort from me," she said to him, "I have always shown my face from the day I was born."

He looked at her for a long time and saw that she was very beautiful. The woman bent down, smiled at him and wiped his tears. For the first time in his life, the man felt the softness of a caress on his face.

– Tadjo

CHAPTER 3

The Formation of the Shadow

We spend our life until we're thirty deciding what parts of ourself to stuff into the invisible bag we drag behind us and we spend the rest of our lives trying to get them again.

— ROBERT BLY

THE FORMATION OF THE PERSONA

You will not be able to understand the concept of the shadow if you don't know the concept of persona. This essential component of the personality is also called the "ego-ideal." Since Jung, the term "persona" signifies, more precisely, the social self resulting from all the adaptive efforts we deploy to conform to the social, moral and educational norms of our milieu. The persona rejects from its field of awareness all elements – emotions, character traits, talents, attitudes – judged to be unacceptable by the important people around us. At the same time, as I stated earlier, it produces in the unconscious a counterpart to itself, which Jung called "the shadow." The persona is thus to the shadow what right-side-up is to upside-down.

The Jungian concept of persona originates in the notion of *prosopon*. In Greek theatre this term designated the mask that the actors wore to enable them to become the incarnation of a character. The Latin word *persona* comes from *per sonare,* which means "to resonate through." The actor's mask was used both to project the voice and to illustrate the personality of the character being played. Each *prosopon* represented a type of the human condition, such as jealousy, greed, meekness, and so forth. Thus, the mask did not represent the actor's personal drama, but rather a conflict of a universal nature. However, the actor's voice still conveyed the accompanying emotions and feelings.

Examples of the polarization of the qualities of the persona and the shadow are shown below.

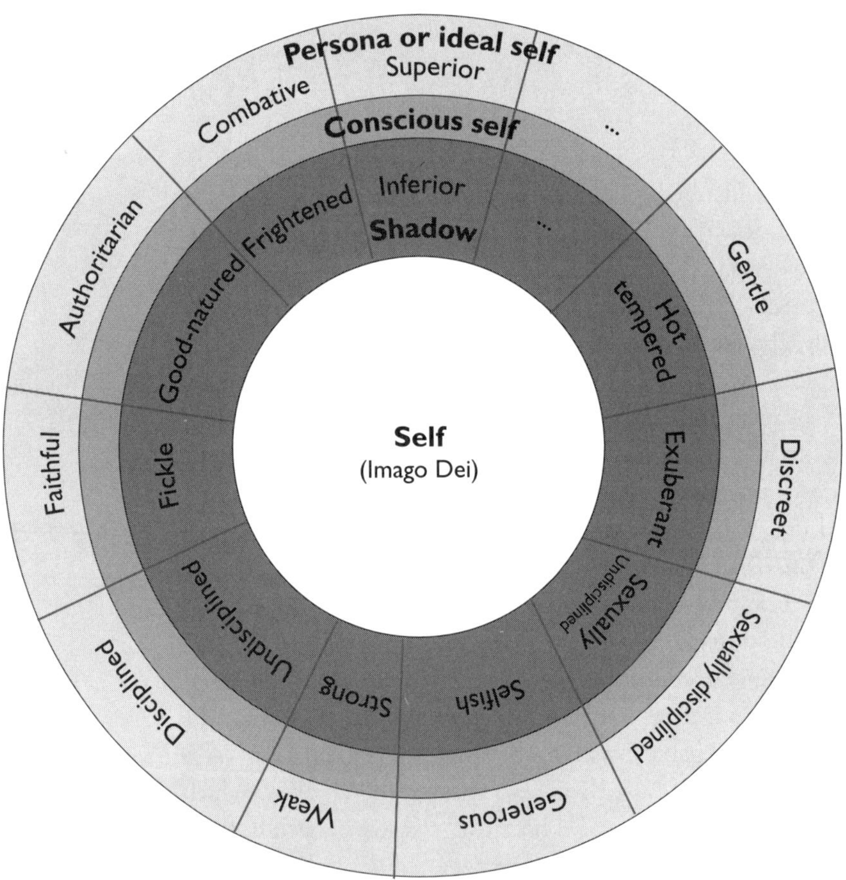

The dilemma of the persona self and the intimate self

When the persona self tries to adapt to the surrounding society, the intimate self loses importance.

As people's persona develops, it simultaneously creates a problem for them: by playing the various roles imposed by their different social milieux, they risk concealing their true identity. In other words, people's efforts to conform to the "appropriate" behaviours required by whatever groups they belong to, and their efforts to play the roles and adopt the values taught by those groups, lead them to lose their own originality (their "inner voice," to use Erich Neumann's expression). Without going so far as to speak of a total loss of identity, we need to recognize that the activity of the persona creates a radical opposition between the social self and the intimate self. When the persona self tries to adapt to the surrounding society, the intimate self loses importance. There is thus a danger that this intimate self will take refuge in the shadow in order to leave as much room and energy as possible for the persona, which is continually concerned with adjusting to the outside world. This led Jung to say, in keeping with existing spiritual wisdom, "The mask does not know its own shadow."

At this point, we face a problem which, at first glance, seems insurmountable: we must adapt to our surroundings, without neglecting the growth of our intimate self. A tall order! On the one hand, we must promote the development of the persona or risk crippling a person's socialization process; on the other, we must preserve the growth of the person's intimate self by curbing the amount of energy devoted to social adaptation. Just how can we achieve this?

Helping the child build a social self ...

It is important to stress here the need to build, first and foremost, a healthy and solid social self (a persona), even if it

The need to construct a social self necessarily brings with it the formation of a shadow.

means having to do shadow work later on. However, some authors contend that a perfect education should be able to eliminate any shadow formation in the child, so that once the child reaches adulthood, the burden of the shadow will be non-existent. They believe that this socialization process that the self undergoes is responsible for the harmful formation of the shadow zone in the personality.

Both Robert Bly and Alice Miller think this way. These writers compare a child's potential for growth to a sphere that tries to open out freely in all directions at the same time. They imply that any prohibitions encountered would block the child's spontaneous growth and create a harmful shadow. This view bears a strong similarity to the utopian thought of philosophers like Jean-Jacques Rousseau. According to Rousseau, the child's perfect nature is corrupted when it comes into contact with society as represented by parents and teachers.

In my opinion, it is unrealistic to expect that a child can develop without the involvement of parents and teachers to curb certain instinctual and narcissistic tendencies that would interfere with socialization. To ignore a child's sociological context – the world of family, society, culture – to protect them from any societal influence would be the equivalent of imposing on that child a universe which is completely closed in on itself, like that of the autistic child.

We cannot choose to have or not to have a shadow. The need to construct a social self necessarily brings with it the formation of a shadow. To believe we can educate our children while avoiding this phenomenon is an illusion.

… without creating too much shadow

The ideal development of the social self – or the development of the ideal persona – should take place by virtue of a flexible and reasonable adaptation to the social norms and values of our milieu. The child's socialization should be so directed that the deepest aspirations of the intimate self are respected as much as possible. To this end, wise teachers will discipline a child's behaviour, taking care to recognize, first, the emotions, the instinctual tendencies and selfish inclinations present. While needing to restrict the child's inappropriate behaviour, such teachers must also avoid forcing the child to repress the accompanying emotions and feelings. In fact, teachers can forbid an angry child to hit a friend and at the same time acknowledge that it is legitimate to feel angry. Two things will thus be achieved: the child will not unduly repress their anger, and the child will have an incentive to come up with positive ways of expressing it.

The child's socialization should be so directed that the deepest aspirations of the intimate self are respected as much as possible.

PERSONA AND FALSE SELF

The function of an individual's persona, then, is to allow us to adapt to the requirements of our social context and enable us to behave accordingly. But adapting to our environment creates problems at times. It can cause the formation of the false persona or what Winnicott calls the "false self."[12] This pathology develops in the primary relationship with the mother. Children who are too frustrated adapt to the maternal world defensively. Because they are unable to make sense out of the mother's or teachers' reactions a lot of the time, their only option will be to defend themselves against a world that they find intrusive or threatening. Such circumstances end up arresting the normal development of the social self (the persona). These children will construct a persona that eventually gives rise to social problems. This abnormal adaptation, far from being useful to the conscious self, actually contributes to its alienation. The false self stops

Individuals who thus create for themselves an iron-clad persona no longer dare to express their true feelings and emotions.

trying to adapt to its environment in the normal manner, instead doing everything possible to protect itself from a world that it experiences as hostile.

Individuals who thus create for themselves an iron-clad persona no longer dare to express their true feelings and emotions, but manifest only those they believe are acceptable to their teachers. In applying this strategy, which Transactional Analysis calls "racket feelings" (a kind of trafficking in feelings), children have the impression that they can survive in an environment perceived as nasty and hostile.

The experience that originally triggered this defensive reaction in the child explains the behaviours by which children seek to manipulate the environment to their own advantage, as Eric Berne, the founder of Transactional Analysis, describes so subtly.[13] But this lack of authenticity comes with a price. When someone has not managed to adapt to their milieu in a normal fashion, the false persona will be the root cause of a particularly virulent shadow deeply embedded in the unconscious.

FORMATION OF A VIRULENT AND DISSOCIATED SHADOW

To understand more precisely the nature of the shadow, think of it as made up of various constellations, each constituting a "psychic complex." Each complex is made up of an organized set of images, words and emotions, forming an independent structure that is dissociated from the conscious self. Each such complex forms a "sub-personality" that could be compared to a character in a play – autonomous, independent from the director and claiming its own personality. These complexes often appear repeatedly in the subject's dreams. Without actually creating a multiple personality psychosis, they nonetheless exert such an influence that the dreamer sometimes literally feels possessed. Saint Paul deplored this aspect of the human condition as he experienced it in himself: "For I do not do the good I want, but the evil I do not want is what I do." (Romans 7.19)

Not all of my clients' shadows possessed the same degree of virulence and psychic autonomy.

All shadows are not equally virulent

I have learned from my clinical practice that not all of my clients' shadows possessed the same degree of virulence and psychic autonomy. Why? Apparently it depends on the circumstances surrounding the past trauma and the repression of the psychic material.

Suppression and repression

Psychoanalysis distinguishes between two forms of personal inhibition. The first is called "suppression." It results from voluntary inhibition of an emotion or an attitude. As suppression is conscious, considered and voluntary, it does not normally create a shadow in the subject.

The second form of inhibition is called "repression." This consists of rejecting psychic potential without even being aware of it. Repression may be further divided into two types: the first arises due to a lack of opportunities for development; the second, as the consequence of a psychic wound.

As examples of the first type of repression we might look at people who, for various reasons – ignorance on the part of their teachers, lack of opportunity or a hostile environment, to name only a few – were unable to use all their potential. The shadow that stems from this untapped potential will, like a child who has been locked up in a cell for many years, have a primitive and undeveloped nature rather

The virulent and "dissociated" character of certain shadows is hard to explain.

than an aggressive one. On initial contact with society, such children will appear rough, wild and confused, for they do not know any of the basic rules of life in society, never having learned how to talk, wash, eat or, in general, behave in society.

The second type of repression results from strict taboos that have been imposed by someone's surroundings. In this case, the person's psychic energy is pushed back into the depths of the unconscious without them even being aware it is happening. The nature of the shadow that results from this type of repression will be marked by virulence and autonomy. Such subjects do not recognize the shadow as their own, and have the impression that this psychic complex is totally foreign to them. They see their shadow as something "dissociated" from themselves, and at the same time, find themselves unable to control it. People struggling with this kind of shadow will sometimes have the impression of being "possessed" by an outside force that they cannot master.

Identification with the aggressor

The virulent and "dissociated" character of certain shadows is hard to explain. To date the best explanation I have been able to find is that not only the psychic content of the repression has to be taken into account, but also the manner in which it was repressed. When a prohibition is imposed violently, the subject-victim is inclined to adopt the behaviour of the one who imposed the prohibition. This can be recognized as the classic case of the victim's tendency to identify with the aggressor and, subsequently, to imitate them. Although it is difficult to explain the mechanism through which this imitation occurs, the victim is inclined to appropriate the gestures, words, tone of voice, violent attitudes and silence of the aggressor. In short, the wounded person's shadow unconsciously takes on the characteristics of the one who inflicted the wound.

Robert Bly maintains that each time we repress an emotion, a quality, a character trait or a talent, it is as if we were throwing these parts of ourselves into a garbage bag.

Consequently, persons thus wounded will be tempted to perpetuate the aggression they themselves suffered – through self-accusation and self-blame, and even self-mutilation. Moreover, they will sometimes experience a compulsive need to attack people close to them. As unconscious prisoners of such a virulent shadow, these persons will be condemned to live a life that alternates between fits of masochism and sadism. Here lies the origin of the violent acts and sexual perversions that therapists observe in certain patients.

The shadow as a garbage bag

To illustrate how the shadow is formed, American poet and thinker Robert Bly uses the telling metaphor of the garbage bag. He maintains that each time we repress an emotion, a quality, a character trait or a talent, it is as if we were throwing these parts of ourselves into a garbage bag. According to Bly, during the first thirty years of life, we are busy filling the bag with rich elements of our being. Over time, the bag becomes heavier and heavier to carry. Consequently we must spend the rest of our lives rummaging through it to recover and try to develop aspects of our person that were stuffed away there.

Recycling the contents of the bag requires humility and patience. If we do not commit to this task, we will eventually feel crushed by the weight of the bag. First we will feel lethargic, as if we're marking time; then we will experience a huge inner void and, finally, become depressed. The precious elements of our being that were rejected and stuffed into the bag, far from remaining inactive, will continue to bubble up, wanting to disclose themselves and break through. Gradually, the psychic energy imprisoned in the bag will take revenge

Why do people drive such a wealth of potential back into their unconscious? They want to survive in a milieu that prevents them from being themselves.

against its owner, creating a mountain of obsessions within or, externally, projecting itself onto those around us.

Why is the garbage bag so full?

Why do people drive such a wealth of potential back into their unconscious? They want to survive in a milieu that prevents them from being themselves; they fear being excluded socially if they give in to being themselves. Whether real or imagined, this fear takes on various forms: fear of losing the affection of our parents, family and close friends; fear of being isolated; fear of feeling marginalized by the group; fear of being ridiculed; fear of being embarrassed; fear of being wrong or abnormal; fear of failure; fear of being considered eccentric.

Some prohibitions at home and at school

To illustrate the damage done by this fear of rejection, a few examples follow of children who, more or less consciously, had to inhibit the expression of their emotions, qualities, character traits or talents.

One father always became very nervous and tense and flew into a great rage when his children were having fun and making noise. The children understood very quickly that they had no right to act like children, to run or shout or play. The father's strictness originated in his own childhood, which he had not been allowed to enjoy because his mother had burdened him with very heavy responsibilities from an early age.

In another family, where everything had to be shared in common and done together as a family, the children began very early on to suppress any form of affirmation of their individuality, such as being able to enjoy a space of their own, spend time alone in their room or have their own secrets.

In yet another family, any sign of affection, tenderness or intimacy was forbidden for fear it might turn into sexual thoughts or play. But at the same time, without realizing it, the parents were fostering behaviour that was cold, distant and sometimes even contemptuous towards other people.

Every family is inclined to accept the expression of certain feelings and emotions and to reject others.

Every family is inclined to accept the expression of certain feelings and emotions, and to reject others. In one home it's acceptable to show fear, pain or weakness but not strength, independence or radiant health. In another, the opposite is true: it's acceptable to show you are strong and in good health, but not that you are dependent, ill or suffering.

Sometimes teachers snub students who appear less gifted or learn more slowly. These students understand quickly that they cannot let on to such teachers that they have not grasped something by asking questions or taking the time they need to solve a problem.

In a religion class, students admitted they did not dare to show their notebook to their parents, particularly not the prayers they had made up. They feared their parents mightn't care or would ridicule them.

The opinion of their peer group takes on great importance for children and adolescents. A young boy, for example, decides not to use the correct forms of language he has learned from his parents because he is afraid that if he does his peers will call him a "mama's boy." Similarly, a young girl won't do beautiful drawings because she fears her friends will become jealous.

A studious young man is harassed by classmates who cannot forgive him his brilliant comments in class and his academic success. It won't take him long to learn that by appearing less intelligent, he can escape such taunts.

A boy won't let himself cry when he hurts himself if he

The major transitions in life are often sources of repression.

fears he'll be considered a "sissy." He might try to hold back his tears even to the point of not feeling the pain.

Although she might really want to play like the boys, this young girl makes sure she is not caught climbing trees. She does not want her teachers to think of her as a tomboy. She suppresses the slightest manifestations of the "masculine" side of her character.

Repression during certain major life transitions

The major transitions in life are often sources of repression. During such transitions, whether they result from some trauma or from a conversion experience, people are often obliged to make radical changes. Therefore they try to forget and deny what they were in their previous life and tend to stuff into their "garbage bag" precious acquisitions from that life.

Having claimed for themselves a new life, these people try in vain to forget their entire past with both its giftedness and its shortcomings. This creates a very long and burdensome shadow. Take, for example, the fundamentalist attitude of certain religious converts who condemn themselves for their past religious indifference. Instead of integrating into their new life the "pagan" side that haunts them, they try to shed it. Some alcoholics do the same thing when they try to toss into their shadow their entire past as alcoholics. This is why many of them are so intolerant of any alcohol consumption, even a "normal" level.

The wife of one of my clients deserted him because of his repeated fits of anger. After his divorce, he swore he would never lose his temper again. Instead of feeling at peace with this resolve, he felt constantly assailed by the fear of falling into his old ways again. Because he had not befriended his anger, it became an obsession.

Nor can we free ourselves from a troubled period of personal history by repressing it. To give one more example, a committed mother of a family was certain she had done with her former life of prostitution. But she was constantly haunted by the fear that others were criticizing her past. Moreover, she had never managed to forgive herself for it. Only after she had been able to be reconciled to the "prostitute in her" could she live at peace with herself.

I would like to examine a series of prohibitions relating to our expression of certain emotions, qualities, character traits and talents.

Other prohibitions

The list of situations that cause us to repress parts of ourselves could be very long, but I'll stop here. Now I would like to examine a series of prohibitions relating to our expression of certain emotions, qualities, character traits and talents. Of course we are dealing here as much with real prohibitions as with words and actions that are interpreted as such by the person involved.

When you read this list, perhaps you will recognize yourself. This new awareness will let you make an inventory of the repressions your shadow is sheltering. During this process, you will note that the simultaneously absolute and negative character of these prohibitions increases their inhibiting power.

Prohibitions about becoming yourself

• Being forbidden to grow up or to change, to think about yourself, to draw attention to yourself, to be a man or a woman, to be healthy or to be sick, to take time for leisure, to be original, to be loved for who you are or to be proud of yourself, to be alone, and so forth.

These are the kinds of prohibitions that often diminish your awareness of your personal giftedness and your ability to develop it.

Prohibitions about emotions

• Being forbidden to express emotions such as fear, jealousy, anger, tenderness, sadness, etc.; being forbidden even to think about having certain emotions; being forbidden to be sensual or to enjoy sexual pleasure; being forbidden to feel "small" and vulnerable, etc.

Prohibitions about learning

• Being forbidden to experiment, to learn, to not know or to feel stupid; being forbidden to distinguish yourself from others by your talents such as drawing, dancing or eloquence; being forbidden to be competent, to feel incompetent, to make mistakes, to be intelligent or intellectual, to succeed, to have faith, to express your faith publicly...

Prohibitions about intimacy

• Being forbidden to create bonds of friendship, to have an intimate life, to show your affection in words or in actions, to love someone of a different race, to trust...

Prohibitions about self-confidence

• Being forbidden to ask or to refuse, to express your opinion, to have projects, to be conservative or "cutting edge," to use your own judgment to distinguish between being helpful and annoying people; being forbidden to be proud of yourself, to say you are lovable or capable, and so forth.

You may well have found the list of prohibitions you just read irritating and even unbelievable. But think about it. These are the kinds of prohibitions that often diminish your awareness of your personal giftedness and your ability to develop it. If you want to tap into these riches stuffed away in your unconscious, one day, humbly, patiently and courageously, you will have to dig deep into your "garbage bag," retrieve your "prohibitions" one by one and give yourself permission to use them.

However, many will be afraid to explore their shadow, for psychic material suppressed in the unconscious for years tends to regress and become violent. The primitive, wild and rebellious character of the shadow not only frightens the individual, but gives the impression that the shadow is a moral evil to be avoided. It is a grave mistake to think this way, as we shall see later on in this book.

Many will be afraid to explore their shadow, for psychic material suppressed in the unconscious for years tends to regress and become violent.

THE WOLF OF GUBBIO

The inhabitants of the Italian village of Gubbio were proud, if not arrogant, people. Their village was clean: their streets were swept, their houses freshly whitewashed and their orange roof-tiles well-scrubbed. The old people were happy, the children disciplined, the parents hard-working. From their village, perched on the side of the mountain, the people of Gubbio looked with scorn on the plains villages. They considered "the people from down below" dirty and not to be associated with.

Now it happened that in the dark of night a shadow made its way into Gubbio and devoured two villagers. The entire population was filled with consternation. Two brave young men offered to go and kill the monster. Armed with their swords, they waited for the enemy with determination. But in the morning, the people found only their mauled bodies.

Total panic gripped the villagers. They knew this was the work of a wolf who was roaming their streets at night. To rid themselves of the problem, the village council decided to call on a holy man known for his ability to talk to animals – none other than Francis of Assisi. A delegation set out to meet with Francis to implore him to come and chase the wolf out of their peaceful village forever.

On the way back, the holy man left the delegates at an intersection and went off into the forest to talk to the murderous wolf.

The next morning all the villagers had gathered in the public square and were getting impatient with how long Francis was taking. When they finally saw him emerge from the forest, they began to shout with joy. Walking slowly, the saint made his way to the fountain, climbed up onto it and spoke harshly to his listeners: "People of Gubbio, you must feed your wolf!" Without another word, he got down from the fountain and left.

At first, the people of Gubbio did not take this well at all. They were angry with Francis. Their fear of the wolf gave way to disappointment and then to anger against this useless saint. But, thinking better of it, they appointed one villager to put a leg of lamb outside his door that night. And they did the same every night after that.

From that day forward, no one in Gubbio was ever attacked by a wolf again. Life returned to normal. And the people had become much wiser through this ordeal. They dropped their arrogant and scornful attitude towards the plains people. The presence of a wolf in their lovely village had taught them humility.

Welcoming Your Shadow

You cannot know a thing
unless you know its opposite.
You cannot become sincere
unless you have experienced
hypocrisy and decided
to fight against it.

– Abu Uthman Maghrebi

THREE WAYS OF UNDERSTANDING THE UNCONSCIOUS: FREUD, NIETZSCHE, JUNG

Jung considered the reintegration of the shadow to be the ultimate moral challenge. This work consists of recog-nizing our shadow, accepting it as part of ourselves and reintegrating it into the whole of our personality. Those persons who can welcome and embrace their shadow become whole and unique individuals.

For Sigmund Freud, the unconscious is a world of chaotic forces always ready to burst the fragile boundaries of our conscious.

To achieve this reintegration of the shadow, Freud, Nietzsche and Jung suggest approaches that differ according to how they understand the nature of the unconscious and the relationship between it and the conscious self.

For Sigmund Freud, the unconscious is a world of chaotic forces always ready to burst the fragile boundaries of our conscious. It is like a volcano, churning with the instinctual and erratic drives of the libido, threatening to erupt at any moment. The conscious, because of these potential explosions, needs to create a strong defense system for itself. To offset the libido's drives, Freud advocates arming the conscious with two main defenses: education in "the reality principle" and solid intellectual development.

In Nietzsche's view, on the other hand, there is no need whatsoever to defend ourselves against the unconscious. While recognizing the chaotic and irrational nature of the unconscious, he rejects Freud's negative view of it, and praises and favours its spontaneity. He exalts the unconscious powers, not only of the Superman but also of the subhuman, even with its evil tendencies.[14] The Nazis were able to use this kind of thinking in a distorted way to justify their racist and destructive instincts.

Jung moves away from both these extreme positions. For him, the unconscious is a set of opposite but complementary forces that need to be organized. It consists, first of all, of apparently contradictory forces like those of the ego and the shadow, the masculine and the feminine, and an infinite number of archetypal polarities. These forces are responsible for psychic tension that is constantly fluctuating. However, the polarizing activity of the Self tries to organize all these opposing elements into a coherent whole (see diagram on page 63).

The Jungian understanding of the development of the

person stresses the need to establish the right balance between the elements of the psyche. Harmonizing the conscious ego with the shadow, which Jung defines as "the totality of the unconscious," is particularly important. Jung thinks that these two psychic entities must maintain their opposition within a balanced system, by means of a dialectic that favours this tension. This process brings to mind the Taoist vision of the real: the universe results from the constant and invisible harmonizing of its fundamental polarity, the yin-yang.

The Jungian understanding of the development of the person stresses the need to establish the right balance between the elements of the psyche.

According to Jung, it is also very dangerous to overvalue or undervalue either one or the other aspect of the psyche. Anytime we promote one at the expense of the other – the ego at the expense of the shadow, for example, or the other way around, we introduce into the psyche an imbalance that eventually translates into physical ailments or mental problems.

THREE PITFALLS TO AVOID IN SHADOW WORK

Jung believed that psychological health consisted, in part, in maintaining the right psychic balance between the ego-ideal (persona) and the shadow. To understand what he meant, let us look at the harmful effects of promoting one of these components at the expense of the other.

Identifying with your ego-ideal and excluding your shadow

What happens to a person who identifies exclusively with their ego-ideal: that is to say, with their persona? As a result of this identification, that person denies not only the impulses of their shadow, but also its very existence. Moreover, this identification requires strict adherence to the behavioural codes of a social group. Fearing that even the slightest violation of these codes will result in their exclusion from society, they experience uncontrollable anxiety. They will be so busy figuring out the real

Perfectionists can never sustain the amount of effort necessary to keep their shadow from emerging.

or imagined expectations of the group and managing their social image that they will end up having to let go of fulfilling their legitimate aspirations.

The perfectionist is an example of this phenomenon. Unable to stay in touch with and express their "feeling" side, they try to hide their weaknesses for fear of being caught out. Always on the alert, they are afraid of committing any mistake in their work or in their relationships. They are perpetually in a state of stress. Their intransigence towards both themselves and others, and their moral, spiritual and psychological rigidity, therefore surprise no one.

In the long run, perfectionists can never sustain the amount of effort necessary to keep their shadow from emerging. The resulting psychic tension provokes all sorts of painful reactions: obsessions, uncontrollable fears, prejudices, and compulsive moral lapses, to say nothing of the psychological fatigue and depression they experience.

This psychological type might be compared to the person presenting "the following traits: poor self-esteem, rigid thinking, narrow-mindedness, dogmatism, anxiety, pronounced ethnocentrism, religious fundamentalism, conformism, prejudices, lack of creativity," individuals whom theologian Richard Coté describes as "intolerant of ambiguity."[15]

At first glance, this is a pretty desperate picture. But remember the saying "It must be good for something." Depression sends the depressed person a clear signal that change is in order and that they must stop identifying with their ego-ideal. This phenomenon is even more evident in mid-life, when the shadow's demand for recognition becomes more insistent. People will then recognize that the time has come to make room for the shadow that they have been trying in vain to conceal.

Identifying only with your shadow

Consenting to become your shadow condemns you to live a life controlled by your passions.

Another untenable way of resolving the persona-shadow tension is to favour your shadow side and obey its impulses indiscriminately. People who opt for this solution soon fall prey to their own shadow. They adopt deviant, instinctual, primitive, infantile and regressive behaviours, to describe just some of the undesirable actions in which they engage. Life in society proves impossible for them, for they give free rein to all their desires, be they sadistic, envious, jealous, sexual or whatever. In short, consenting to become your shadow condemns you to live a life controlled by your passions.

I cannot help but mention here the deplorable effects of certain therapies that claim to enable individuals to fulfill themselves by eliminating every form of inhibition from their lives. Those who have been initiated into such practices often become incapable of forming or maintaining good relationships with those close to them, of working as part of a team or co-operating with authority. We saw this in the seventies, when certain initiates of primal scream therapy were rendered incapable of living with their families or getting along with their colleagues. Their only hope of having a social life lay in getting together with other individuals on the fringe of society who had been involved in the same type of therapy.

Robert Louis Stevenson's novel *The Strange Case of Dr. Jekyll and Mr. Hyde* illustrates well the danger of identifying exclusively with our shadow side. The hero, Dr. Henry Jekyll, succumbs to the progressively spellbinding power exercised by his shadow. By drinking a potion he himself has concocted, the generous doctor is gradually transformed into Edward Hyde, a sordid character. After his first attempts to identify with his shadow, that is to say, his alter ego Hyde, Jekyll begins to realize the danger he is courting. He hastens, therefore, to justify this double-identity

Doctor Jekyll's fundamental mistake was his recklessness in agreeing to become his shadow.

adventure that could, he suspects, lead to his moral decline. He tries to convince himself that he is carrying out this experiment in the name of science and, to still his conscience, he calls this transformation "harmless." He goes so far as to see in it nothing more than "gaiety of disposition." Indeed, he derives a certain pleasure from his dangerous visits to his alter ego, and he tells himself that, at the very worst, these visits could lead to some innocent pranks.

John Sanford, a Jungian analyst, provides a penetrating analysis of this story. His commentary on the work shows that Dr. Jekyll's fundamental mistake was his recklessness in agreeing to become his shadow. Instead of trying to establish a fruitful tension with his alter ego, Jekyll refused the discomfort of his situation and chose to lose himself in Edward Hyde.[16] This is the reasoning of those who choose a decadent lifestyle, saying that the best way to get rid of temptation is to succumb to it.

To the extent that Jekyll agrees to become Hyde, he yields progressively to the demands of his dark character. His repeated resolves to end the matter – including his willingness to take up religious practice again – do not achieve his liberation from Hyde's hold over him. Thus, he reaches a point of no return, where all moral sense and all self-mastery elude him. Henceforth he is at the mercy of diabolical forces against which he can do nothing. Powerless to resist his sadistic impulses, he murders his colleague, the good Dr. Carow.

Dr. Jekyll's risky undertaking illustrates well how abandoning ourselves to the drives of our shadow can only lead to decline. This attitude fails to resolve our inner moral tension and does not promote the reintegration of the shadow.

Identifying alternately with the ego and the shadow

In everyday life, rarely do we encounter cases as extreme as those of the "perfectionist" or Dr. Jekyll. The third – and more common – pitfall is to lead a double life. In these cases, individuals usually lead a morally exemplary life. Their reputation as a model spouse, parent and citizen are the envy of all. Then fatigue or depression sets in. At that point, they let themselves take liberties with their moral principles. These temporary lapses in conduct vary a great deal, both in their forms and in their degree of seriousness: romantic escapades, sexual adventures, fits of anger, excessive drinking, small crimes, slander, gossip, and so forth.

Most alcoholics know this type of yo-yo pattern well: under the influence of alcohol, their sober and exemplary ego is completely bowled over by their alcoholic shadow.

For a moment these people are seduced by temptation; then they get hold of themselves, regret their mistake and resolve to change – until they succumb again, that is. They are caught in a vicious circle. This reminds me of the case of a priest who had a reputation for untiring devotion. After periods of intense work, he would succumb to one of his dark sub-personalities under whose influence he would engage in inappropriate sexual behaviour. For several years, he alternated between periods of generosity and periods of sexual deviance.

Most alcoholics know this type of yo-yo pattern well: under the influence of alcohol, their sober and exemplary ego is completely bowled over by their alcoholic shadow. It's like witnessing a split in their personality. It is amazing to see in their alcoholic side qualities that are opposite to those in their sober side: in their inebriated state, gentle people reveal their violence; those who are models of sexual restraint suddenly throw caution to the winds; stingy people show their generous side; and atheists are drawn to pray.

People who are tossed back and forth in this way between the aspirations of their ego and the impulses of their shadow are liable to remain locked in a vicious circle, and periodically sink into a psychological and spiritual slump.

You can't escape the dilemma of the ego-ideal versus the shadow.

HOW TO MANAGE YOUR ENCROACHING SHADOW

Be responsible for the tension between the ego and the shadow.

You can't escape a dilemma by eliminating one side of it. The same applies to the dilemma of the ego-ideal versus the shadow. It is a question of assuming and holding the tension that the dilemma creates. At first, the subject will feel caught and torn between these two apparently irreconcilable and even contradictory realities. But those who persist in this uncomfortable state will see their deep self, their Self, taking charge of bringing these poles into harmony; the opposites will show themselves to be complementary.

Writers who have dealt with the life of the psyche from a spiritual and symbolic perspective have given the dramatic confrontation between the ego and the shadow various names. It will suffice to mention a few. The alchemists called it nigredo; the mystics, the night of faith; the myths of Osiris and of Dionysus described it through images of dismemberment of the person; shamanism speaks of breaking into pieces and of cooking in the cauldron. Elsewhere, initiation rights describe the ego-shadow conflict in the symbolic form of a torture or a burial. More familiar to some is Christianity's comparison of it to the death of the old person and to a crucifixion.

At some point during our psychological and spiritual growth, the day comes when each of us finds ourselves up against unacceptable emotions and feelings as well as strong instinctual and irrational drives. We must learn to neither give them free rein nor suppress them. We need to simply recognize that these movements within us are part of our internal dynamics and accept them, without trying to cure them. This welcoming attitude, which neither releases nor represses, fits with the teaching of Zen philosophy on dealing with anger: refrain from acting when overcome by anger, but be sure not to suppress it; befriend it by welcoming it.

Those who succeed in reconciling the dualities encountered in their existence stand a strong chance of achieving spiritual harmony.

Throughout our life, the shadow is continually splitting up psychic entities that want to be harmonized. Jungian analyst Robert Johnson[17] maintains that to transcend apparent opposites by cultivating a sense of paradox constitutes inestimable progress for our consciousness. Many people live according to polarities: they either love or hate; express their emotions or suppress them; work or relax; give of themselves generously or look after themselves; are in relationship or are isolated; are active or are contemplative. But those who have developed a paradoxical vision of the world come to see these apparent opposites as complementary.

Furthermore, maintaining a dualistic mentality causes considerable harm to our spiritual development. Any spiritual progress must be rooted in a vision that harmonizes the apparent opposites of reality. It follows that those who cannot resolve their emotional inner conflicts – opposing drives, conflicting responsibilities, apparently contradictory values, etc. – are condemned to spiritual sterility. On the other hand, those who do succeed in reconciling the dualities encountered in their existence stand a strong chance of achieving spiritual harmony. This prompts Robert Johnson to conclude that the art of transforming contradictions into paradoxes belongs to the symbolic function of religion. He believes that developing a sense of paradox will allow us to reach a higher state of consciousness.[18]

The question is this: How do we go about attaining this level of consciousness?

A feeling of powerlessness will overcome those who try to get out of this situation solely by the rational, determined efforts of the ego.

Bringing the ego-ideal and the shadow into harmony by appealing to the Self

To escape the discomfort of psychic tension, some people adopt a heroic posture shaped purely by reason and will. But such a posture cannot be sustained over the long term. However, a certain kind of heroism is called for: the ability to bear the tension created by two opposite tendencies, which sometimes resembles a form of crucifixion. A feeling of powerlessness will overcome those who try to get out of this situation solely by the rational, determined efforts of the ego. The diagram on the next page shows the organization of the opposing qualities of the persona and the shadow around the Self.

Organization of the opposing qualities of the persona and of the shadow around the Self

In these circumstances, the only recourse is to abandon ourselves to a higher psychic authority: the Self. Jean Houston, my religious anthropology professor, liked to remind us that in our moments of breakdown we could go beyond ourselves (breakthrough).

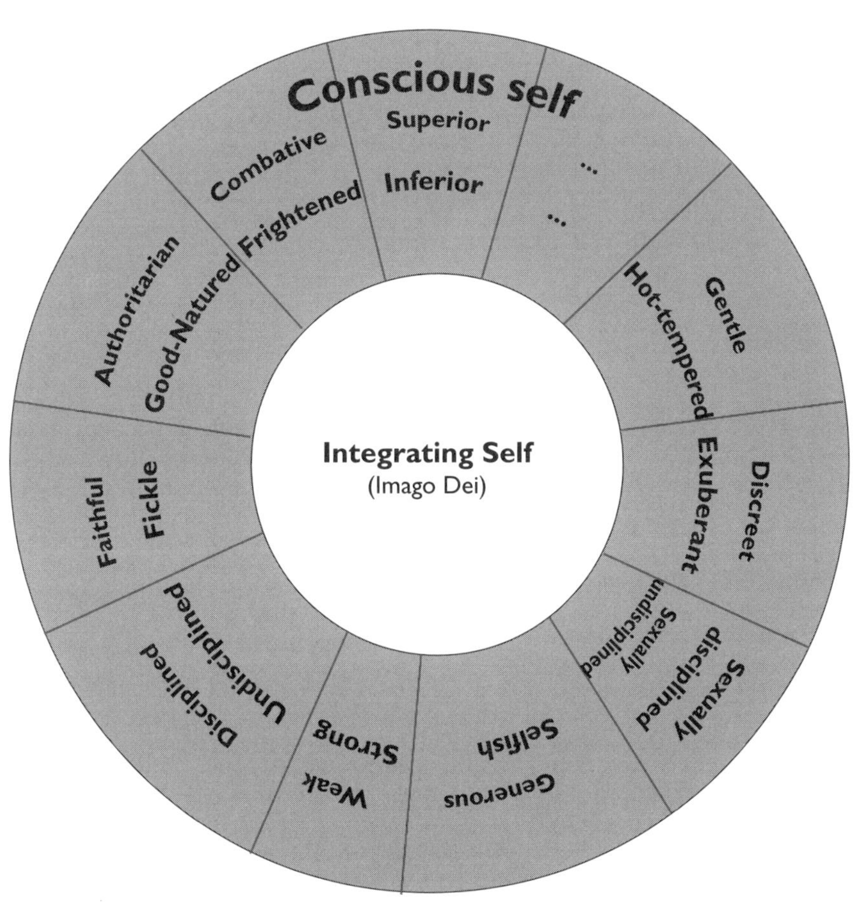

Once a person has consented to being crucified between their ego and their shadow, the Self comes to the rescue.

Who is this Self (or deep self) that is called to play such a determining role in reintegrating the poles of the psyche? Jung sees in this Self the *imago Dei* or the divine principle present in the heart of every individual. He also sees there the creative and integrative centre of the person, which intuitively possesses the overall plan for an individual's growth. The Self intervenes to organize into a harmonious whole these conflicting psychic elements. How does it accomplish this integration? By evoking transcendent symbols that can appease the spirit and bring unity to contrary psychic forces. Later I will examine how religious symbols play this unifying and harmonizing role.

Once a person has consented to being crucified between their ego and their shadow, the Self comes to the rescue. The Self offers a form of resurrection, a transformation of the self through the reconciliation in progress. For Jung, this transformation marks the beginning of the individuation process. Taking the disparate and opposing elements of the psyche, the Self creates a new internal organization of the person, offering a new insight into the complexity of our being. This event brings with it a greater maturity; I become more myself and surer of the resources I carry within. Apparent contradictions in my being and behaviour are resolved into a superior harmony, and I enter an idyllic period when the fiercest of antagonists are able to live side by side. The Old Testament prophet Isaiah poetically describes this state of grace that characterizes messianic times: "The wolf shall live with the lamb, the leopard shall lie down with the kid, the calf and the lion and the fatling together […]. The cow and the bear shall graze, their young shall lie down together; and the lion shall eat straw like the ox." (Isaiah 11.6-7)

Transcending the source of conflict between the ego and the shadow

Sacrificing the ego

To be open to the influence of the divine Self, the ego must be… prepared to be sacrificed.

To resolve the tension we just discussed, the ego must first let go. In this situation, it will tend, however, to be afraid and to strengthen its control over the personality. But to be open to the influence of the divine Self, the ego must be able to drop this rational and self-determining attitude. It must be prepared to be sacrificed: that is, to abandon its claim to be the psychic centre and its desire to manage everything from its point of view.

This symbolic death of the ego brings to mind the image of the grain of wheat that falls to the ground, of which Jesus speaks in the gospel: "Unless a grain of wheat falls into the earth and dies, it remains just a single grain; but if it dies, it bears much fruit. Those who love their life lose it, and those who hate their life in this world will keep it for eternal life." (John 12.24-25)

By dying to itself, the ego acquires a totally new vision, that of the Self: evil is conquered; life is reborn from death; divine love resurrects what was lost.

The wise person anticipates and fosters this apparent disintegration of the self which is so full of promise. But generally, people postpone taking the necessary measures, unaware of the change that has started to take place in them. Then there is danger that a negative event (like illness, failure, bankruptcy, being fired or overworked) will trigger a destabilizing confrontation between the person's ego and their shadow.

The polarizing action of the Self

To read certain authors, you would think that the thrust towards transcendence that takes us beyond the categories of good and

To sacrifice your ego, you must abandon yourself to the wisdom and integrating power of the Self.

evil and the various dualities just happens naturally, as if by magic. Simply sacrificing the ego is all it takes to guarantee your salvation. What they don't mention is how hard it is to actually do this. To sacrifice your ego, you must abandon yourself to the wisdom and integrating power of the Self. This requires great courage and deep confidence in the healing and integrative power of the spiritual centre of our being.

To succeed in this undertaking, we need to combine psychological and religious efforts. The psychological balance sought in overcoming the ego-shadow dichotomy depends on giving up the Self's position of control in favour of the "transcendent function" of the Self – to use Jung's expression. This function of the Self produces unifying symbols that permit and point to new psychic syntheses. Thus, in the sacred space of the psyche, an activity takes place that may be termed "religious." As the etymology of this word– *religare,* to bind together – suggests, the role of this activity is to bind, that is, to reconcile psychic opposites such as masculine and feminine, love and power, suffering and salvation, loss and gain, action and contemplation, ownership and poverty, freedom of choice and duty, etc.

Sacred symbols emerge at this time of reintegration

We have just seen how the work of reconciling the ego ideal and the shadow begins with a veritable crucifixion and is then transformed into a resurrection through the action of the Self. When sacred symbols rise up within our consciousness, it can perceive this reconciliation concretely. These symbols begin to appear in our dreams, during psychological and spiritual exercises, and when we are engaged in artistic activities. They signal that a deep psychic transformation has begun. (Incidentally, the very roots of the word symbol – *sun bolè,* "to place together" – suggest this process of integration.) Furthermore, the great religious symbols, such as the cross, the mandala, the Tai-Chi-Chu (yin-yang), the flower (lotus, rose), and the mandorla, to name but a few, have the same effect on the psyche (see the following illustrations).

During an exercise to integrate the ego and the shadow, fourteen of the twenty participants said that a sacred image was present in their mind or that they had some type of religious experience. The emergence of sacred symbols within us signals a new and deeper level of consciousness of our being as well as the birth of a new unity. The active presence of these symbols during artistic activity, in mental imagery or in dreams indicates the arrival of an inner liberation and a broader understanding of ourselves.

Tai-Chui-Chu (yin yang)

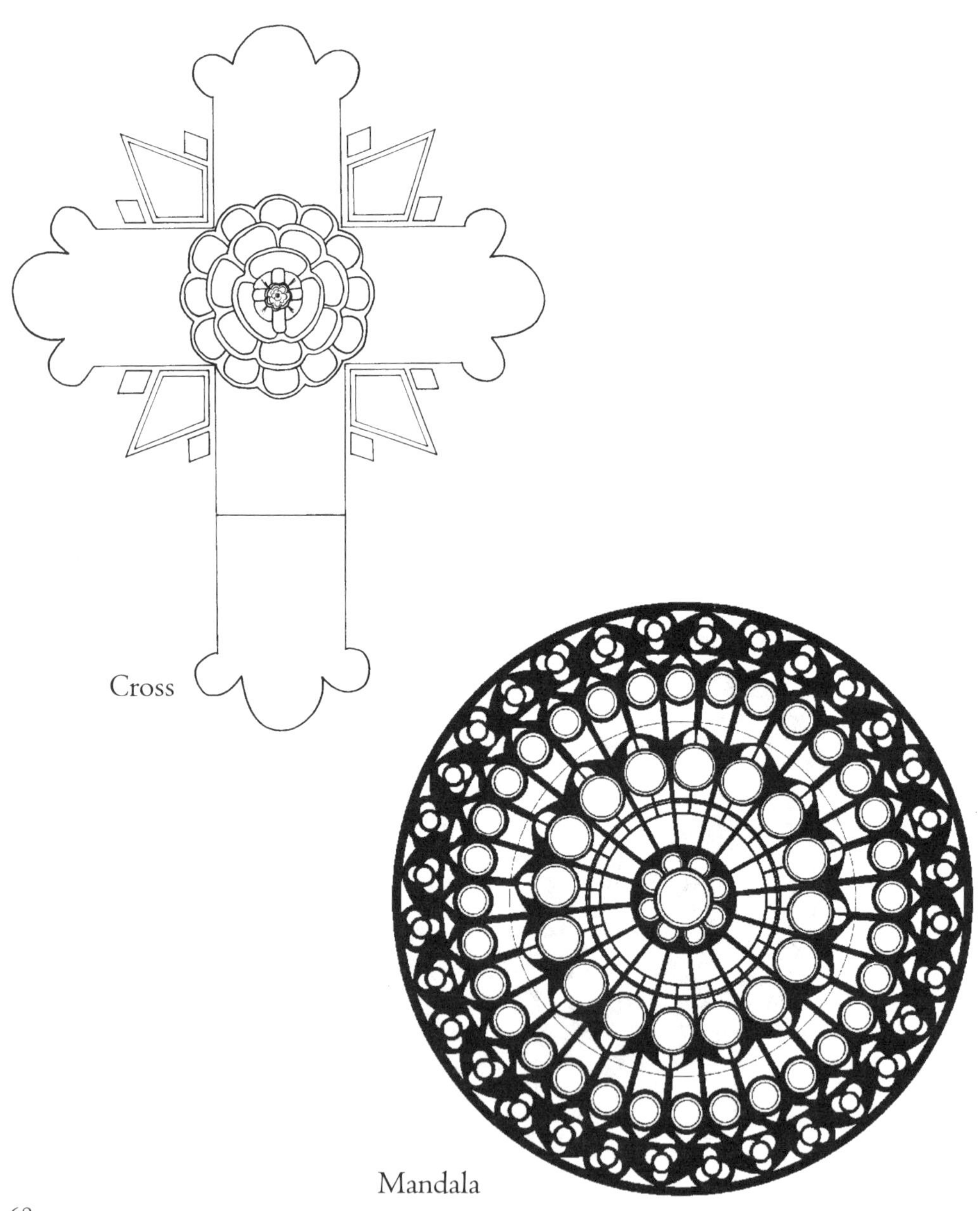

Cross

Mandala

Mandorla

Flower

The emergence of sacred symbols within us signals a new and deeper level of consciousness of our being as well as the birth of a new unity.

At the same time it is a sign that we may expect healing from illness, mental disorders and spiritual dryness. Persons blessed by this kind of inner revelation see their own individuality, their own unique way of being an image of God, gradually being realized within them. They acquire a deep awareness both of themselves and of their calling in the world.

To conclude this chapter, let us re-examine the legend of the wolf of Gubbio. Saint Francis of Assisi personifies the Self. He entreats the arrogant villagers not to fight their wolf – that is, their shadow. Rather, he invites them to accept the wolf as one of their own, to treat it well by feeding it. Thus, instead of being a threat to the village, the wolf will become an integral part of it. Its constant presence will help the villagers to be less scornful and arrogant and, henceforth, humbler and more genuine.

THE STORY OF THE LOST WALLET

One beautiful summer evening, a man looked out his window and saw his neighbour on the street, crouched down on his hands and knees. He seemed to be looking for something under the street lamp. So the man said to himself, "I'm going to help him find whatever he's lost."

He went over to his neighbour and asked him, "What did you lose?" The other replied, "I've lost my wallet. And what I'm most upset about is not the money in it, but all my identification and credit cards."

Our good Samaritan started searching too, around the lamppost, on the sidewalk, on the road, on the adjacent lawns. After much fruitless effort, it occurred to him to ask, "Are you sure you lost your wallet around here?" Naïvely, his neighbour answered, "Oh no, it wasn't here. I lost it in the field over there." The man couldn't believe his ears. How could his neighbour expect to find his wallet under the lamppost when he had lost it somewhere else? Intrigued, he asked him to explain why he was looking here. With all sincerity came the reply, "Well, it's quite simple: the light's much better over here."

CHAPTER 5

Recognizing Your Shadow

I am not me
I am the one who walks by my side
whom I don't see
The one whom I visit sometimes
and forget other times
The one who forgives me
when I eat candy
The one who walks in nature
when I am indoors
The one who remains silent
when I speak
The one who will stand tall
when I die

– JUAN JIMENEZ

LOOKING IN THE RIGHT PLACE

The toughest task facing those who wish to befriend their shadow is precisely that of looking for it in the right place. What makes this search all the more challenging is the shadow's distinctive ability to hide in the unconscious. Like the hidden face of the moon, the shadow remains unknown, obscure and mysterious.

DENYING THE EXISTENCE OF YOUR SHADOW

Before we can meet our shadow, we need to stop denying its existence. We are generally so good at ignoring our shadow that this component of our being remains masked. It is important, then, to acknowledge its presence in us and to accept it as an integral part of our personality, despite its obscure, elusive and mysterious nature.

The following nine questions will enable you to make out the shape of your shadow.

In a style all his own, R.D. Laing describes how difficult it is to notice our shadow even though it constantly influences us:

> The range of what we think and do
> is limited by what we fail to notice.
> And because we fail to notice
> that we fail to notice
> there is little we can do
> to change
> until we notice
> how failing to notice
> shapes our thoughts and deeds.[19]

Is our shadow completely elusive? Are we condemned never to get to know this side of ourselves? How can we come to know it so we can embrace it and reintegrate it into our consciousness? These are the questions this chapter addresses and seeks to answer.

STRATEGIES FOR RECOGNIZING YOUR SHADOW

In this section, I am proposing a set of strategies that can help you recognize how your shadow makes itself known, and get a clearer and more accurate picture of it.

I. Discover the hidden side of your personality using a series of questions

The following nine questions will enable you to make out the shape of your shadow. Why so many questions? Because you will need several converging answers to successfully identify the various facets of your shadow.

Question I

The first question has two parts:

• What are the most flattering aspects of my social ego, those traits that I would like others to recognize?

Then ask yourself:

• What are the opposite qualities or traits that I have had to repress to highlight my positive traits?

This question touches on the social image that you wish toconvey to those around you. Let's take an example: if you want to come across as a gentle, generous, smiling person, most probably you have to hide your aggressivity, your selfishness and your angry outbursts. These character traits that you have repressed make up the various facets of your shadow.

If you're brave enough to do so, identify with the various aspects of your shadow and say, for example, "I'm aggressive; I'm selfish; I'm bad-tempered." Pay attention to the emotions that rise up within you as you say those words. People react in very different ways. Some will say, "I feel confused"; others say, "I feel guilty and ashamed"; still others say, "I feel energized."

Question 2

• What topic(s) of discussion do I tend to avoid in my conversations with people? Sexuality, aggressivity, faith, ambition, incompetence… ?

Whatever it is, you can be certain that avoiding them reveals your fear of uncovering a side of yourself that you are ashamed of. Unless you completely trust your conversation partner, you will feel very ill at ease broaching these subjects. The day you manage to tackle these topics, preferably with a discreet listener whom you trust, you will have already succeeded in befriending one aspect of your shadow.

Question 3

• In what kinds of situations do I find myself becoming nervous, over-sensitive and defensive? What type of remark would startle me?

Are you surprised at how strongly you react? If so, this is an indication that someone has just stepped on a part of yourself that you do not accept. Your level of discomfort and your extreme reaction are evidence that a sensitive part of your shadow has just been sideswiped.

The same is true for a group. The embarrassed silence of a group following a comment by one of its members signals that the hapless party has just broached a taboo subject. In other words, the remark has partially unveiled the collective shadow. It's like talking about rope in a family where there's been a hanging.

Question 4

• In what situations do I feel inferior or lacking in self-confidence? Do I feel this way, for the most part, when I feel that I'm not equal to the task at hand, or that I can't live up to what the situation requires because I can't see myself as competent, articulate, intelligent, discreet or _______ enough?

At one point during my career, I found myself in a group of people, most of whom were artists. I had a hard time understanding why I was constantly uncomfortable until I realized that in my life I had not only neglected but in fact had repressed all artistic expression.

Question 5

• In what situations do I feel embarrassed? In what field do I panic at the idea of allowing someone to see my weakness? Do I feel embarrassed if someone asks me point-blank to carry out some sort of activity, like speaking or singing in public?

People who are grieving come to mind here. They can only express emotions such as sorrow, anger, guilt and helplessness. Rare are those who dare to say that they feel liberated when someone they love dies, particularly if caring for that person during their illness was very demanding.

Question 6

• Am I inclined to be offended when someone criticizes me? What kinds of criticism do I find annoying or even irritating? A violent reaction to a remark signals once again that some facet of your shadow has just been exposed. If you always react that strongly to recurring criticism from those close to you, it means that they are exposing a hidden side of your personality that you really don't want to show.

Another hypothesis could also explain this kind of extreme reaction: you have become the group's scapegoat. Then you need to ask yourself what in you could have made the people around you choose you as the repository of their shadow.

Question 7

• Do I find it difficult to accept a compliment?
If someone pays you a compliment, such as "You look very elegant," "You're really creative" or "You do things so well," you reject it because you see no grounds for it, you think you should give the credit to others, or you want to play down its importance. In this instance you would do well to probe your reactions: "Why do I invest so much energy in defending myself against these signs of admiration? Am I not trying to camouflage a part of my shadow, namely, an ardent desire to be admired that I don't admit?"

Question 8

• In what respects do I feel upset or dissatisfied with myself? For example, am I unhappy with my physical appearance or a particular character trait?

If so, you are probably trying to conceal something that you consider a weakness. Alternatively, your persona may be imposing on you impossible ideals of success, beauty or perfection and, consequently, you may be forcing yourself to repress anything that does not seem to match these ideals.

One thing is definite: accepting your imperfections, your weaknesses, your shortcomings and your mistakes will show that you have begun to befriend your shadow. This is the beginning of the wisdom called humility.

Question 9

• What quality did my family value most as I was growing up? Every family presents a characteristic trait. So, people would say about the Monbourquettes, "They're honest, decent folk"; about the Robinsons, "They have a lot of courage"; about the Smiths, "They're hard-working people"; about the Lucianos, "They're so hospitable."

To identify your family shadow, you only have to go to the opposite quality from that one prized by your family's milieu. For example, to maintain its reputation of "honest decency," a family would have to renounce any recourse to shrewdness and diplomacy; to maintain a reputation of courage, any manifestation of fear would have to be repressed; to keep being seen as hard-working, they would have to deprive themselves of all leisure; to continue their practice of hospitality, they would have to give up their family boundaries.

The family shadow, then, will be whatever the family did not allow itself to live and express.

The family shadow will be whatever the family did not allow itself to live and express.

II. Analyze your dreams

Jung may be the first to have used the term "shadow" to designate the sinister character that comes to haunt us in our dreams, but Freudian psychoanalysis had already shown the dream as the privileged place for people to meet their shadow. In fact, it attributed to dreams the function of compensating for social behaviour. The unconscious thus allowed itself unbridled expression of all that was repressed by politeness or what we have internalized of society's prohibitions.

According to Jung, the shadow that inhabits our dreams usually takes on the form of a character of the same sex as the dreamer, exhibiting a sinister, threatening, repulsive or hostile manner. It is often ugly, sick or deformed. Sometimes, the shadow takes the shape of a ferocious animal: a snake ready to bite, a rabid dog, a wild lion… . Dreamers often have the sensation of being chased, threatened or even attacked by their shadow. They will then seek to flee, hide or fight back. Such dreams indicate to dreamers that an important aspect of themselves that has remained hidden until then wants to manifest itself.

Dreams in which the shadow actually attacks – especially if these attacks are recurrent – warn the dreamer of the urgent necessity to take their dark side into account and let it emerge into consciousness, where they can finally welcome it as an integral part of their being. If dreamers ignore these repeated warnings, they are exposing themselves to all kinds of dangers: accidents, illness, depression and relationship problems, to name just a few.

It is important to be well disposed towards your shadow, to acknowledge its presence and to respect its messages. This

My shadow warned me of possible dangers that I was able to avert.

attitude will let you observe the manifestations of the shadow, even if they are fleeting and furtive. Moreover, precisely because the shadow's manifestations are transient, some people consider them nothing more than wild imaginings that don't deserve any attention.

Examples of Dreams

To illustrate this, here are some dreams that feature typical shadow characters. They will provide you with an opportunity to learn to work on the hidden side of your being.

My brother, my shadow

The frequent appearance of my brother, Mark, in my dreams told me of the active presence of my shadow. He often chased me, trying to attack me, hit me or make me fall. During one of these dreams, which I considered to be a premonition, my brother chased me in a car at high speed. To avoid being knocked down, I rose about thirty metres into the air. When I woke up, I had the sensation of still being suspended in the air. A few days later, I had a serious car accident. When I ended up sprawled out on the floor of the car, unhurt but covered in bits of glass, I heard a voice say to me, "Well, you've landed without getting killed!" After that, every time my brother appeared in a dream, I would pay special attention to the message he was sending me. I became increasingly convinced that my shadow knew more than I did about how my life was unfolding. On two more occasions, my shadow warned me of possible dangers that I was, however, able to avert.

Gradually I understood the reason for this phenomenon. During my childhood and adolescence, I hadn't wanted to resemble my older brother in any way. I thought this would enable me to escape the animosity my father felt towards

Mark and, at the same time, channel all my father's affection and confidence towards me alone. To avoid being like Mark, I also had to develop character traits that were totally opposite to his. I hasten to add that, since our reconciliation before he died, I have never seen him in my dreams again.

Meeting the cobra

In another dream, I saw myself pinned down by a cobra that was getting ready to bite me. I woke up with a start, still gripped by fear. I immediately jotted this dream down in a notebook before it could slip from my memory. Then, during a daydream, I asked the cobra why it wanted to attack me. Without hesitation it replied, "I want to destroy you because you are too much of a pacifist and not enough of a fighter." I soon understood its message, which concerned painful situations I did not know how to handle. Then I negotiated with the cobra in the following manner: I would hand over to it my pacifist spirit in exchange for its fighting spirit. I benefited from this exchange. Shortly afterwards, I felt within me the energy and courage I needed to deal with my problems and avoid the professional burnout that was threatening me.

The helpful witch

Here is another dream that illustrates well the shadow's wisdom. A woman religious, whose community had instructed her to withdraw from the project that she had founded, asked to meet with me. She had had to let go of a job that meant a lot to her, one to which she had devoted twenty years of her life. By nature submissive, she believed she had accepted her superior's decision well, and did not appear to be making a big deal out of the deep disappointment this abrupt career change had caused.

The shadow that presents itself in our dreams as our enemy is later transformed into a precious ally.

During our meeting, she told me about a dream that had really intrigued her. She was in a shopping centre with some other nuns. Going down the escalator, she noticed at the very bottom a moving black shape. Gradually, the shape became clearer until she recognized it as having the features of a witch. She froze with fear. Once at the bottom of the escalator, she noticed a piece of black clothing lying on the ground. As she bent down to pick it up, she was astounded to discover that it was the witch's cape. She drew back in terror and dropped the garment. Then she went off to join her companions, who didn't seem to have noticed anything.

When she woke up, she felt that she had had a dream that held a certain significance for her, but she could not figure out how to interpret it. During our session, I invited her to replay her dream. Despite the revulsion she felt, she agreed to play the role of the witch. She felt great anger rise up within her. She became very animated and radiant with energy. I advised her to pursue her identification with the witch by pretending to put on the cape that she had received from her. She was astonished to observe that the cape fit her very well and that she felt very comfortable in it. The metamorphosis that she had agreed to undergo put her in contact with both her repressed anger and her inner power. The exercise of replaying her dream in an awake state to complete it no doubt spared her from an eventual depression.

Many times I have been able to observe that the shadow that presents itself in our dreams as our enemy is later transformed into a precious ally. But for this to take place, we must have the courage to agree to meet it, listen to it, get to know it and, finally, befriend it.

Accepting sexual orientation

A shadow that erupts in a dream does not necessarily have a fixed form. It may well change from one dream to the next. By examining our dreams closely, it becomes possible to detect how our relationship with our shadow is developing. This is clearly illustrated in the story of a young man who had strong homosexual tendencies. This person was so unaccepting of his homosexual orientation that he hated himself. This attitude of rejection was reflected in his dreams, where he saw himself beating a young man who had made sexual advances towards him. With the help of therapy, he gradually learned to accept his homosexual side and, what is more, he came to appreciate the feminine, delicate side of his personality. In a later dream, rather than treat the young man harshly, he surrendered to his amorous overtures. This dream indicated that my client had been reconciled to his homosexual orientation.

Like our inner musings or our moods, fantasies and daydreams represent breaks in the shadow's boundary, which allow it to rise up into our consciousness.

III. Be attentive to your fantasies and daydreams

Being attentive to our fantasies and daydreams, which we don't usually take time to think about, is another way of getting to know our shadow. Like our inner musings or our moods, fantasies and daydreams represent breaks in the shadow's boundary, which allow it to rise up into our consciousness. To become aware of the elements animating this inner world, you must let these phenomena unfold spontaneously: competitiveness, bursts of energy, desire for wealth, sexual impulses, feelings of envy and jealousy, mounting frustration, and so forth. They pop in and out of our mind so quickly that they elude us. Often our conscience finds them unacceptable because of their immoral, base or even cruel or violent nature. Whatever they are, they no doubt signal the active presence of the shadow.

Daydreaming can manifest our repressed mission that we may not recognize otherwise.

The shadow, however, conceals not only negative elements but also positive elements, such as creative inspiration and impulses towards good. The white shadow, which we sometimes tend to forget, also occupies an important place in our daydreams and fantasies. For example, we find ourselves daydreaming about artistic performance, athletic feats, or heroic and virtuous actions that we have performed. Daydreaming can manifest our repressed mission that we may not recognize otherwise.

IV. Examine closely the nature and content of your humour

It has been said that humour is "the shadow's truth." Examining the content of our humour and our reactions to various forms of humour enables us to identify the nature of our shadow. When we laugh at our neighbour who is caught in an embarrassing situation, we often feel the need to apologize for our laughter and insist that we didn't intend the least bit of malice. We say, "I'm just laughing because it's funny," or perhaps, "Please don't take it the wrong way; it was just a joke." In reality, this laughter is not as innocent as we would like to make it seem.

If we look more closely, we see that this laughter often originates in our repressions. It helps defuse the tension between our wanting to be perfect and the inclinations repressed by the superego. Just think of the snickering – or even the roaring laughter – provoked by someone being clumsy during a solemn ceremony, by a dignitary who trips and falls, or by a speaker who has a momentary memory lapse during a serious speech.

Spontaneous humour betrays the presence of the shadow and its cluster of thoughts, desires and fantasies repressed in everyday life. It betrays the side of ourselves that we consider unacceptable to those around us. We know we are wrong to laugh at the poor fellow who slips on a banana peel or gets a cream pie in the face. Nevertheless, a part of us can't help but rejoice at another's humiliation, not only because we're relieved that we're not the ones in the embarrassing situation, but also by virtue of this sadism that lurks in the innermost depths of our shadow.

Spontaneous humour betrays the presence of the shadow and its cluster of thoughts, desires and fantasies repressed in everyday life.

To best use humour for getting in touch with your shadow, ask yourself these questions: What kinds of situations are most likely to make me laugh? In what areas of human activity am I most likely to find humour? The answers to these questions will reveal the repressed sides of your personality.

On the other hand, the shadow of a person who has no sense of humour is so deeply buried or so well armoured that it cannot manifest itself even through laughter.

V. Examine what you project onto others

Freud called dreams "the royal road of access to the unconscious" *(via regina)*; I could just as easily say this about projections: they are the royal road of access to the shadow. Given the importance of this subject, I decided to devote the entire next chapter to it.

HOW TO RECOGNIZE SOMEONE ELSE'S SHADOW

You also need to be able to detect other people's shadows so they won't be able to project their shadow onto you.

Reactions to a remark

If a remark you make upsets or irritates someone, you have probably hooked one of their shadow zones. However they

The shadow is also expressed in the things we forbid others to do.

might attempt to hide this side of themselves, the violence of their reaction has given them away. During a therapy session, a psychologist ventured to offer his client an opinion he had formed of him, based on his observations: he believed he detected some suicidal tendencies. This interpretation made the client very angry: he vehemently denied having any suicidal thoughts. But the psychologist did not back down from his interpretation. The client left slamming the door, and never returned to this psychologist, whom he considered to be rude.

A while later, I accepted this man into therapy. He told me of his unfortunate experience, asking me not to take the same approach as his previous therapist. Nevertheless, during the course of our meetings, he admitted to me that he sometimes wished for a heart attack that would liberate him from the tensions accumulated over a lifetime of setbacks. His first therapist's interpretation had been accurate in that it revealed the client's unconscious desire to die. However, he had erred in not respecting the protest that came from the client's conscious self. While this man's moral upbringing forbade him to have any thoughts of suicide, his shadow, on the other hand, had considered the possibility.

How we forbid something

The shadow is also expressed in the things we forbid others to do. You don't need to be a great psychologist to recognize a father's shadow when he warns his daughters not to sleep with boys, or a mother's shadow when she tells her son not to steal candy bars from the convenience store. These prohibitions reveal their authors' resistance to the impulses of their shadow more than they show concern with sound upbringing. Without realizing it, many educators, by negatively phrasing their instructions or advice, drive children to go against their own moral teaching. It would be so easy to give rules of behaviour expressed positively rather than in the form of a prohibition.

Preachers who take pleasure in vilifying the sexual indiscretions of their listeners make the same error. Does the vehemence with which they speak not betray their personal struggles with their own sexual impulses? Nor is it surprising that certain of these preachers who most ardently denounce sexual permissiveness have themselves been found guilty of sexual misconduct. Their sermons were more of a reflection of their own conflicts with their shadow than of their concern to teach sound moral or spiritual doctrine.

Any work on our shadow begins by acknowledging its existence.

Blaming and criticizing others

Here is one last method of discovering someone else's shadow: listen to the blame and criticism that they direct at others. Ken Wilber comments on this subject: "Our carping criticisms of other people are really nothing but unrecognized bits of autobiography. If you want to know what a person is really like, listen to what he says about other people."[20]

In conclusion, remember that any work on our shadow begins by acknowledging its existence. The intellectual understanding of the shadow helps us begin to see its presence in us. Then a more practical understanding teaches us to welcome this "enemy within" and, gradually, to transform it into a friend.

THE STORY OF THE WOODCUTTER WHO HAD LOST HIS AXE

A woodcutter was looking for his axe. When he realized he had lost it, he began looking where he had last used it, but could not find it.

Little by little, an idea came to him: someone had stolen his axe. His suspicion came to rest on his neighbour's son.

He began to keep a close watch on the young man's behaviour. The more he watched him, the more his suspicions were confirmed: this boy was a thief. His facial expression was not open, there was something odd about his appearance and his timid manner betrayed a dishonest streak. To sum up, he had the expression of a thief, the look of a thief and the manner of a thief. Our woodcutter was just waiting for the right moment to unmask him.

Now, one day, while crossing a lot where he had done some woodcutting, he stumbled over an object: it was his axe. He was perplexed by this discovery. Although he no longer regarded the boy as a thief, he nevertheless continued to bear him ill will.

CHAPTER 6

Owning Your Projections Again

The unloved parts of ourselves which we try in vain to remove from our lives project themselves onto others, forcing us to recognize them.

– John Monbourquette

THE INFLUENCE OF SHADOW PROJECTIONS

Becoming aware of what we project onto others is the royal road of access to the elusive reality of our shadow. Failing to recognize our projections blocks our inner growth and social development. We alienate ourselves from the elements of our shadow that we project onto others and, consequently, deprive ourselves of knowing our resources. If we do not master the art of recovering our projections, we turn in on ourselves. The aspects of the shadow attributed to others will turn on us, prompting states of anxiety and depression, and becoming the source of numerous problems and conflicts in our human relationships. In short, every unrecovered projection becomes a kind of self-mutilation, in which we turn our own psychic energy against ourselves.

We can, however, learn to recognize and neutralize the harmful influence of shadow projections. If we learn to reintegrate them into the conscious zone of our being, they will provide us with an invaluable knowledge of our dark side and, at the same time, will foster a new harmony between our shadow and our conscious side.

To my knowledge, there is no more reliable and efficient test for finding out what qualities and character traits are missing in our growth than the examination of our projections. Indeed, if we are inclined to disdain and detest certain qualities or character traits in others, it is because we have an urgent need to develop these same traits in ourselves.

This process of reintegration of the shadow evokes one of the principles of homeopathy, "Like cures like."

For instance, if I can't stand a gentle, calm and reserved person, there is no doubt that I am lacking these qualities which I need to balance my over-aggressive personality, my agitated manner and my desire to make an impression. First I will certainly need to overcome my reluctance to become gentle, calm and modest: that is, to resemble someone whom I dislike intensely. But once I overcome my initial feelings of revulsion, everything I can learn from this person will help me acquire greater maturity.

This process of reintegration of the shadow evokes one of the principles of homeopathy, "Like cures like," according to which an illness is cured through the application of a tiny dose of the drug that in a healthy person would produce symptoms of the disease.

I will address two main themes in this chapter. First, I will analyze the phenomenon of shadow projection; second, I will describe the stages through which we must go to recover the elements of our shadow that we have thus projected.

WHAT DOES IT MEAN TO PROJECT YOUR SHADOW ONTO SOMEONE ELSE?

A projection story

This true story will help you better understand the phenomenon of projecting your shadow onto someone else. The names of the people involved have been changed.

Adrian, a university professor, never misses an opportunity to trash his colleague, George, for incompetence in both teaching and research. Adrian is on the lookout for any and all gossip on the subject. He delights in recounting George's difficulty relating to his students. He subjects George's writing to microscopic scrutiny in the hope of finding errors, even if they're only minor spelling mistakes. At times, Adrian himself is surprised at the zeal with which he pursues the defamation of his colleague.

Projection is both a psychological and a spiritual phenomenon.

Sometimes it seems to Adrian that the other professors feel ill at ease when he makes his disparaging comments. He is astonished that they can be so blind. He can't understand why they don't see George's professional weaknesses, which are obvious to him. Sometimes he even suspects they're siding with George.

Adrian is not aware of his own fear of being labelled incompetent. Even just thinking about being unable to meet the standards of the profession increases his anxiety. This is why he makes George the scapegoat. By drawing attention to George's shortcomings, he believes he can escape his own anxiety and make people forget his shortcomings.

Adrian's desire to ensure his reputation as an excellent professor is preventing him from seeing his own professional weaknesses. He has banished to the faraway realm of the unconscious even the thought that his work might not be perfect. He feels an urgent need to criticize in his colleague what remains hidden in his own shadow.

George, meanwhile, can't help but hold Adrian in great disdain for his rigidity at work and his lack of humanity. As this situation illustrates, it is in fact rare for a projection to be unidirectional. Adrian and George are caught up in a movement of mutual denigration, always at each other's throats, as if locked in a hostile grip.

Projection theory

Projection is both a psychological and a spiritual phenomenon. Aware of the scope that an in-depth study of this question could entail, I will limit myself here to presenting the Jungian understanding of it. Marie-Louise von Franz, a famous disciple of Carl Jung, defines projection, in the footsteps of

Projection enables me to see, hear and feel emotions, qualities and traits that lie repressed within myself through their resonance outside myself.

her teacher, as "an unconscious, that is, unperceived and unintentional, transfer of subjective [repressed] psychic elements onto an outer object."[21] In other words, projection enables me to see, hear and feel emotions, qualities and traits that lie repressed within myself through their resonance outside myself. Thus, psychic material is displaced from inside me to outside me.

Psychoanalysis sees projection as a primary defense of the conscious against the possible excesses of the unconscious. Psychoanalysis holds that everything that is unacceptable to the conscious will sooner or later be found outside of ourselves, displayed in objects, animals or people.

Von Franz points out that the "projector" – the person doing the projection – is almost always unconscious of both their act of projecting onto others and their projections. They are aware only that they are caught up in intriguing feelings whose object might be either fascinating or repulsive. They will experience attraction if they consider the projected qualities or character traits desirable; they will experience repulsion if they find the projected qualities or traits problematic or threatening. Consequently, in the first case, they will tend to idealize the person on whom they are projecting their feelings and, in the second, to loathe them. In both cases, the projector's appreciation of the person will be distorted, because it will be out of proportion in relation to reality. They will think they are dealing with a reality outside of themselves, while they are actually dealing with one that lives in their own unconscious.

Shadow projections in passionate love

Passionate love provides fertile ground for projections. Because the beloved serves as "symbolic support" for the projection, he or she is endowed with a fascinating side. If the love is reciprocal, there is mutual projection. Passionate love, in fact, feeds on mutual projection of the partners' white shadow.

Once passionate love has cooled,. the daily grind may even imperceptibly turn attraction into revulsion.

During the attraction phase, each partner sees incarnated in his or her beloved the qualities he or she wishes to possess, but cannot access because they are repressed in his or her shadow. In connecting with their beloved, they also have a sense that they are recovering for themselves the desired qualities that they had buried. Someone has joked that it is easier to marry someone with the qualities we would like to possess than to strive to acquire them. The lover who is calm, affectionate, careful with money, and bohemian will be inclined to fall in love with one who is dynamic, reserved, generous and conventional. In passionate love, opposites attract.

In passionate love, fascination is capricious. But once passionate love has cooled, the situation does an about-face. The daily grind may even imperceptibly turn attraction into revulsion. The lover's personality has not changed; rather, the initial fascination has turned into fear. In fact, as sexual attraction diminishes, old fears, nourished by the shadow, resurface. We are back at square one: that is, the point where we had buried in our shadow everything that might cause us to be socially rejected.

A couple will find that what fascinated them about each other at the beginning of their relationship has now become repulsive. The husband now has the impression that the ideal wife he knew "when they were still in love" has changed in every respect: she is no longer "dynamic" but "hysterical"; not "reserved" but "frigid"; the "generous" wife is now "controlling"; from being "conventional," she has become "stubborn." The wife has the same experience: she sees her husband transformed from a "calm" man into a "boring" one; he has changed from being "affectionate" to a "sex

If this person's impoliteness or tactlessness gets on your nerves to the point where you are repulsed by or even afraid of them, there is reason to believe that you are projecting onto the individual in question.

maniac"; from being "careful with money" to "stingy"; now, he is not "bohemian" but "unpredictable." Their reasons for marrying have become their reasons for separating.

It is not easy for spouses to extricate themselves from the dead-end situation that mutual shadow projection creates, despite its apparent initial benefits. To save their relationship, they will have no other option but to stop blaming each another, take back ownership of their respective shadows and build a new relationship based on mutual respect of each other's personality. All couples have to face this challenge one day if they wish to grow as individuals and as a couple.

Fascination: a characteristic of shadow projection

During a lecture I was giving on the shadow, a member of the audience asked, "According to your theory, then, the observation of a fault or shortcoming in another person is nothing more than the result of a projection?" This question gave me the opportunity to point out the important distinction between an objective observation and a subjective observation that is distorted by the projection of a shadow.

You might observe someone's rudeness or tactlessness without being affected by it. That would be an objective observation. If, on the other hand, this person's impoliteness or tactlessness gets on your nerves to the point where you are repulsed by or even afraid of them, there is reason to believe that you are projecting onto the individual in question. You have exaggerated or blown their impoliteness or tactlessness out of proportion. In them you have observed something that you have not wanted to recognize in yourself and have forced yourself to bury in your unconscious all your life.

The same applies to prejudices. If, for no particular reason, we are prone to ascribing bad intentions to someone or to suspect them without a valid motive, we are obviously seeing reflected in that person a secret part of ourselves that we have so far tried to deny.

History testifies to collective projections that caused atrocious crimes, cruel persecutions and wars.

The harmful effects of projection

The poet and thinker Robert Bly once stated in a lecture that people who are the object of projection face a real danger to the integrity of their personality, and even to their life. Fascination presents the risk that all the adulation will lead them to develop illusions about themselves. Alternatively, in cases of repulsion, they may become the scapegoat to be persecuted. History testifies to collective projections that caused atrocious crimes, cruel persecutions and wars. We have only to think of the witch hunts, in which thousands of women were burned at the stake because they were suspected of conspiring with the forces of darkness.

While perhaps less spectacular, the effects of everyday projections, even positive ones, are equally pernicious. Marie-Louise von Franz compares them to "projectiles." From the time they first hit, whoever is the unfortunate target will feel more vulnerable and more inclined to self-doubt. When other people project positive or negative qualities onto us, this often produces a certain ego-insecurity. We no longer know whether we really have such splendid or such ugly traits or not, especially since there is almost always a "hook" on which the projection is "hung."[22]

What von Franz means is this: in any projection, the one onto whom the qualities are projected offers a hook: that is, one or more traits on which the projection can be hung. For

Loving our enemies does not appear so unreasonable to those who remember that very often we create our own enemies by making them bear the weight of our shadow.

example, if you project your aggressivity onto someone, the person must already be displaying some aggressive traits.

The existence of these troubling effects in parent–child or therapist–client relationships are being increasingly recognized. Although it would be interesting to discuss here the influence of the parental shadow on the child's unconscious, as well as the transference and counter-transference that are so common in therapy, I will refrain from doing so, because a study of these areas would take us beyond the stated aim of this book.

Projection and the creation of enemies

The words of Jesus about loving our enemies are among the most astonishing in the gospels: "You have heard that it was said: 'You shall love your neighbour and hate your enemy.' But I say to you, Love your enemies and pray for those who persecute you." (Matthew 5.43-44) At first, we find such a prescription jarring and unreasonable. Would Jesus ask us to betray ourselves or, even worse, to act like masochists?

But on reflection, loving our enemies does not appear so unreasonable to those who remember that very often we create our own enemies by making them bear the weight of our shadow. When individuals and collective bodies or groups become aware of this and learn to take back ownership of their projections, they will find themselves the richer for it and will discover in others not "enemies" but "neighbours" on whom they will be less inclined to declare war. But as long as they do not apply themselves to this task, they can expect to be victims of their own projections, as this Hindu proverb tells us: "Choose your enemies well because, before too long, you will become like them."

"RE-APPROPRIATING" SHADOW PROJECTIONS

The following examples show four people clearly involved in projection onto someone else.

Can we be "cured" of the projections we cast onto others? By definition, the shadow is a reality of which we catch only fleeting glimpses; by nature, it escapes even the keenest direct perception. At the same time, the fascination and revulsion that accompany it are constant and permanent. Through these emotions we have a good chance of discovering the shadow's movements and their significance. If we approach the shadow from that angle, we recognize that it is possible to be cured of our projections by recognizing their presence within us and reclaiming them.

Below, I use four typical cases of projection to illustrate the usual five stages for re-appropriating our shadow.

Stage 1: Unconscious projection

The following examples show four people clearly involved in projection onto someone else.

1) Mark was raised in a home where peace and quiet reigned at all costs. His mother and father never allowed him to express the least feeling of anger. He had acquired the reputation of being "gentle and kind." Not surprisingly, he chose as his wife a rather combative and domineering woman. His marriage is not going well. He accuses his wife of being a "fanatical witch." His wife reproaches him for being a "wimp" and even a "coward."

2) Isabel, a single young woman of thirty, has finally found a religious group where she feels at home and where her spiritual aspirations are fulfilled. She has placed all her confidence in the guru, who obviously has a charismatic talent for preaching and who advocates certain spiritual exercises to

These four cases feature individuals who have become the victim of the projection of their own shadow.

help his followers "blossom."

3) Gerry had built himself a reputation as a hard worker. He has teamed up with an old acquaintance to start a new company. Now, the more he slaves away to make the business a success, the more he has the impression that his partner is doing nothing. The partner is taking a lot of holiday time to satisfy his passion for golf. When he does show up at the office, too often it is to chat with the employees, making them waste time. Gerry is beside himself and can no longer tolerate this loafer of a partner.

4) Melanie, a very pretty woman with delicate features, married the man who could give her the comfort of financial security and abundant fatherly advice. After a few years of marriage, she stopped seeing in her husband the protective father she had seen at first. All she sees in him now is an oppressive person who reminds her of her own father's domineering attitude.

These four cases feature individuals who have become the victim of the projection of their own shadow. Mark disowned any aggressiveness he might still have had in him and dumped it onto his wife. Isabel saw in her guru her complete spiritual fulfillment. Gerry left it to his partner to see that the need for relaxation was met, while Melanie gave up her financial and psychological independence by projecting it onto her husband.

These individuals find themselves in a difficult, challenging situation. They feel they are at the mercy of another person who seems to be keeping them from living. How can they recover the riches hidden in their shadow? Does the solution lie in separation and flight? Experience has shown that even if these people were to divorce or separate, they would end up choosing similar partners further down the road.

Stage 2: Adjusting the mask created by the projection

Projecting your shadow onto someone else is the same as putting a mask on another person's face and then reacting to the mask.

Projecting your shadow onto someone else is the same as putting a mask on another person's face and then reacting to the mask. The character thus created may either fascinate or repel you. The mask that you thought fit the other person's personality so well does not always fit and could easily fall off. The favourable or unfavourable preconception that you initially had painted of the other person does not always correspond to the actual behaviour of the one bearing the projection.

Mark, therefore, does observe in his wife occasional surges of tenderness and kindness, which blur the image of her that he has constructed for himself. It seems that she is not always the "fanatical witch" he thought he saw in her.

Isabel, although she is totally devoted to her guru, is shocked to learn that he regularly sleeps with the most beautiful women among his followers. Moreover, she has trouble understanding how a man who enjoys such a reputation for being holy can accept gifts of expensive cars he doesn't even use.

Gerry, too, is sometimes surprised to see his lazy partner show interest in the company's business and get through a good chunk of work from time to time.

Melanie is astonished that her husband is not always the tyrant she had thought him to be; in fact, sometimes he is quite gentle and conciliatory.

The "projector" now begins to doubt whether his or her preconceptions are well founded. These moments of doubt provide the opportunity to recognize our projection and correct our false perception of the other person. But, alas, these moments are usually short lived.

It's not easy to drop our projections.

Stage 3: Justifying our extreme judgment of the other to maintain our projection

It's not easy to drop our projections. Even in moments of doubt, we try to convince ourselves, against all the evidence, that the other is indeed as we had judged them to be in the first place.

Mark, the "nice guy" husband, tests his wife's tolerance more often by not letting her know that he'll be home from work late. There are times he forgets (on purpose?) an important birthday or anniversary. His wife loses her temper about his indifference and thoughtlessness. Her aggressive outbursts reinforce his idea of her: a "witch" who's always raging at him.

Wanting to get to the truth of the matter about her guru's unconventional behaviour, Isabel confronts him with the discrepancy between his sermons on the one hand and his sexual behaviour and extravagant luxury on the other. Remaining completely calm, her guru explains to Isabel that once someone has reached a certain level of renunciation, they enjoy complete freedom to "love" everyone and to benefit from the wealth of creation. Mildly satisfied with the explanation, Isabel struggles to continue believing that her guru is a holy man.

To prove to himself that his partner really is lazy, Gerry steps up his efforts to check on him, harbouring a secret desire to catch him wasting time. And, indeed, once in a while, he succeeds in catching him out. That's all he needs to be convinced that his partner is downright lazy.

Melanie, confused by her husband's goodness towards her, decides to attend a feminist lecture, which proves that, from earliest times, all men have been "domineering, phallocratic, total patriarchs." She comes home from the lecture convinced that, even when men are kind, they are really just using a hidden strategy to help them maintain their domination over the female sex.

"Projectors" are prepared to resort to false arguments to justify their condemnations.

So they don't have to let go of their projection, and so they can avoid suddenly having to evaluate themselves by taking into account the reality of their shadow, the "projectors" are prepared to resort to false arguments to justify their condemnations.

Stage 4: Feeling robbed and diminished by the situation the projection has created

If the "projector" is bending over backwards to keep their shadow projected on the other person at any cost, it will not be long before the "projector" suddenly feels robbed, undermined and diminished as a person. It is easy to imagine the enormous amount of psychic energy being used up as the "projector" lets themselves be tossed about by an object that alternates between appearing attractive and repulsive.

The "projectors" will feel diminished for two reasons: first, they will have the impression that they've been deprived of the qualities they have projected onto someone else; this will cause them chronic stress. Second, they will feel tormented by their projections, as if their own psychic energy was turning against them. In other words, they will end up frightening themselves.

Let's take another look now at the four cases described above and examine the disastrous effects that their own projections will have upon each of the "projectors."

Mark, the good guy who shoved all his aggressiveness onto his wife, has a hard time defending himself against her or against anyone else with whom he gets into a conflict. He feels he's just a doormat.

Trying to keep your shadow projected onto someone else will gradually lead to physical exhaustion and psychological depression.

Gerry, who projects onto his partner his capacity to take time out for rest and relaxation, is often on the verge of professional burnout.

Despite her guru's explanations, Isabel continues to feel uneasy about his activities. She becomes increasingly confused and finds herself in a spiritual desert.

Melanie continues to believe she is a victim of her husband. Her self-confidence is slipping and the more she feels dependent on her husband, the more she hates him.

Trying to keep your shadow projected onto someone else will gradually lead to physical exhaustion and psychological depression. You'll feel impoverished and diminished in every respect. You'll live on the defensive, afraid to take risks and inclined to compare yourself unfavourably with others. Finally, you'll tend to blame yourself for not doing anything and, especially, for not being good at anything.

Stage 5: Assuming responsibility for your shadow

Depression often leads the "projectors" to become aware of the abnormal situation they're in and to seek help to get out of it. In that sense, it provides the opportunity to re-appropriate their projections and to build real self-esteem, finally allowing them to affirm themselves in a healthy way.

What happy ending to the story might there be for the four people whose situations we have followed thus far?

Mark stops being afraid of any aggressivity in himself and becomes aware of his ability to assert himself. He learns to reconcile assertiveness and gentleness. This allows him to throw off his burdensome "Mr. Nice Guy" reputation and makes him a more attractive partner for his wife.

Tired of the excesses of her guru, Isabel leaves the sect and agrees to be "deprogrammed" by a specialist. After that, she seeks to rediscover the sources that had nourished her spiritual life in the past.

Gerry has to learn from his business partner to stop taking life so seriously and to relax from time to time. The quality of both his life and his work are much improved as a result.

Instead of wasting her life complaining about her husband, Melanie needs to recognize in herself her masculine qualities of courage, initiative and strength. Thus she befriends all the potential of her masculine side, stops competing with her husband, and now feels that she is his equal.

A German proverb says that you can't jump over your own shadow, which means get rid of it. When you try to eliminate it from your life, it comes back with a vengeance, imposing its presence forcefully in a variety of ways: anxiety, guilt feelings, fear and depression. Such fragmentation reminds me of the gospel admonition that is so apt here: "A kingdom divided against itself cannot last!"

Jesus Christ himself denounced what today we are able to understand as the harmful nature of projections of the shadow.

JESUS CHRIST DENOUNCES UNHEALTHY PROJECTION

Jesus Christ himself denounced what today we are able to understand as the harmful nature of projections of the shadow. His comments on this topic are still relevant: "Why do you see the speck in your neighbour's eye, but do not notice the log in your own eye? Or how can you say to your neighbour, 'Friend, let me take out the speck in your eye,' when you yourself do not see the log in your own eye? You hypocrite, first take the log out of your own eye, and then you will see clearly to take the speck out of your neighbour's eye." (Luke 6.41-42) Thus Jesus expresses in his own way what we have been trying to demonstrate in this chapter: before judging others and thinking our judgment can help

Before judging others and thinking our judgment can help them, we need to think about working on ourselves and learn to reclaim our shadow projections.

them, we need to think about working on ourselves and learn to reclaim our shadow projections.

Jesus denounces malicious projection for he knows its effect on those who are its object. He denounces it in the story of the adulterous woman who is pursued by a group of men. She had just been caught in the very act of committing adultery. The men who brought her to Jesus were making her the scapegoat for their own sexual transgressions. In one succinct sentence, Jesus turns the situation around; he questions them, making them aware of their projection, and invites them to take responsibility for their own faults: "Let anyone among you who is without sin be the first to throw a stone at her." (John 8.7)

Exposing the malevolent projections of others is not without its dangers, for it can bring down on the accuser the wrath of those accused. We only have to look at the fate that Jesus had to suffer.

LOADING MY NEW BOAT

Because I was afraid of damaging my brand new boat, I put only a very small load in its hold. Skittishly, the boat rocked from side to side, heaving so far out of the water that you could see its keel. Light as a cotton ball, it was laid flat in the water by the force of the raging winds. I simply couldn't steer it anymore. To make matters worse, I was getting very little out of these trips.

I decided to increase the size of my load. Then my boat plunged into the sea up to its waterline. Clumsily, it obeyed my commands. I could tell that my boat trips were going to be more rewarding. Then, one day when the sea was rough, my boat began to sink and, for a moment, I thought it was gone. But another boat came to the rescue, and my boat and I made it to shore safe and sound.

Finally, I learned how to load my boat so that it was stable, and I could manoeuvre it and avoid any serious risks.

CHAPTER 7

Strategies for Befriending Your Shadow

It is better to be complete than perfect.

– C.G. Jung

HOW STRATEGIES WORK

The last two chapters have described the various facets of the shadow and presented ways to recognize signs of its presence. This knowledge already constitutes significant progress towards deeper self-knowledge. However valuable it may be, though, this information is not enough to allow us to reintegrate our shadow. We need to rely on strategies that will foster reconciliation between the qualities and traits of our persona and those of our shadow.

Each of the strategies designed to achieve this reconciliation involves two stages: first, presenting the psychic material to the Self and then, letting the Self organize it. During the first stage, the conscious self accepts the responsibility of presenting to the Self the conflicting elements in our personality: that is to say, a facet of the shadow coupled with a facet of the ego-ideal (persona). For example, someone who discovers repressed aggression in their shadow will try to locate its conscious counterpart, which might be the excessive gentleness of their persona. During the second stage, the person will actually present these opposites – the repressed aggressiveness and the conscious gentleness – to the Self as accurately as possible, asking the Self to exercise its power of integration. The conscious, voluntary work, then, is limited to the first stage.

The conscious self trusts the integrative power of the Self, and commissions it to carry out the harmonization of the opposing qualities or traits in the person through the mediation of a unifying symbol.

In other words, the conscious self trusts the integrative power of the Self, and commissions it to carry out the "complexification" or harmonization of the opposing qualities or traits in the person through the mediation of a unifying symbol. If, as in the above example, it is a question of reconciling the aggression of the shadow with the gentleness of the persona, the aggression might take the shape of a serpent and the gentleness the shape of a bird. The Self will integrate them by using an archetypal image, such as a winged serpent or a flying dragon. This creation of unifying symbols that heal is something that those who participate in my shadow workshops experience frequently.

CONDITIONS FOR REINTEGRATING YOUR SHADOW AND YOUR CONSCIOUS SELF

The work of reintegrating the shadow into our conscious side is a delicate psychospiritual task. Its success depends on a number of conditions that need to be defined before we can talk about a strategy for integration.

The first condition is to guard against any hastiness. Exposing too much unconscious material at the outset could leave someone depressed. To illustrate this danger, Jung used the metaphor of the fisherman who didn't load his boat properly. If he overloads it, it is in danger of sinking. If, on the other hand, he doesn't pack in a heavy enough load, he is wasting time and energy.

Therefore, those who wish to "eat their shadow" (i.e., to reintegrate it) are advised to arm themselves with patience. They must respect the incubation period necessary for regaining ownership. When one of my clients became impatient with how long it was taking him to become free from the impulses of the shadow, I asked him how long he thought it would take him to eat a whale. At first my question confused him, but he soon got my message: he would have to "eat" it one mouthful at a time.

In professional practice I have observed great disparities in the pace of shadow reintegration.

A second condition for success, which follows on the first, is to work at exploring and reintegrating a trait of our shadow over a period of time, rather than trying to reintegrate it all at once. Marie-Louise von Franz states that it takes time for the shadow's complexes to break up and form new bonds with the conscious elements. Her experience as a Jungian psychotherapist taught her that certain shadow complexes resist any conscious assimilation.

In professional practice I have observed great disparities in the pace of shadow reintegration. Some people need to accumulate small victories in order to satisfactorily reintegrate their shadow.

The third condition stresses the importance of calling on the participation of the Self so reintegration might be successful. It unfolds this way. Before each integration exercise, I invite participants to prepare for it by centering on their Self and invoking their power of integration. According to their spiritual tradition, each participant chooses their own prayer. Christians might ask for the help of the Holy Spirit; others might appeal to their Inner Guide, their divine Healer, Love or the Wise Person in them and so forth.

Finally, the fourth condition for success is to use the various strategies suggested below *in the presence of a witness-friend who, on that occasion, serves as a guide.* This person encourages and supports you through the difficult portions of the exercise. This support will prove necessary when you are overcome by hesitation or the desire to terminate the experience.

The first strategy consists of acting out a psychodrama during which you enter into dialogue with your shadow.

STRATEGIES FOR BEFRIENDING YOUR SHADOW

I. Dialogue with your shadow

The first strategy consists of acting out a psychodrama during which you enter into dialogue with your shadow. Before anything else, you will need to identify clearly the person who is the object of your projection of your shadow; then, you imagine this person seated on a chair opposite you so that you can have a spontaneous dialogue with them. Some people prefer to write down this exchange of views in a journal. You alternate between playing yourself and the imagined person. The important thing is to stay in contact with both so you get to know each other better during this improvised dialogue. Little by little, you come to understand one another until you manage to come to an agreement. The threatening aspect of the antagonist is transformed into something constructive for yourself.

You conclude the exercise by adopting the role of a referee who comes in to assess the reconciliation work accomplished by the persona and the shadow. At the end, you thank the Self for having fostered the reconciliation of the parties in question.

I had the opportunity to observe the very positive results of this kind of exercise in Elaine, one of my students. She was very apprehensive about her coming academic year because she was afraid of having to face a particular professor. Before she even knew him, she dreaded "his arrogant manner," and had begun to hate him. To try to get out of this dead-end situation, she volunteered to try the exercise described above. For more than two hours she sustained the conversation, alternatively playing her role as student and the role of the professor. She noticed just how much she had projected onto him a power of self-confidence that she had repressed in herself ever since childhood. At the end of the exercise, she was managing to integrate into her conscious self the character trait that she had been ascribing to her future professor, towards whom she now felt more kindly disposed. She was both astonished and delighted at the results.

Personalizing your shadow is another method of reintegration.

After attending a few of the allegedly-arrogant professor's classes, Elaine found that, far from feeling oppressed by his personality, she had developed a pleasant rapport with him.

II. Personalize your shadow and make friends with it

Personalizing your shadow is another method of reintegration. To illustrate it, I would like to share with you a personal anecdote, after which I came to accept the "ignorant-in-me" and to allow it expression.

One year, at the start of a new academic term, I met Agnes, a pretty student who told me how keen and excited she was to be able to take one of my courses. She added that, having read my books and attended some of my lectures, she considered me a great thinker.

In class, she paid very close attention and asked me numerous questions. She thus provided me with the opportunity to demonstrate my knowledge. But after a while, I found myself getting more and more annoyed by her countless, often ill-timed interruptions. One day, I even allowed myself to ridicule one of her questions. She did not appreciate that.

From then on, Agnes' attitude changed completely. She started to ask questions to stump me, which was even more irritating because they had nothing to do with the subject matter I was teaching. As soon as she even moved, before she

I realized that Agnes was a threat to the "know-it-all-in-me."

had begun to ask her question, I was on my guard and felt aggressive. Then I would make offensive remarks in response to her questions. In short, we were involved in frequent and totally pointless confrontations that were harming both our inner peace and the smooth running of the class.

Increasingly embarrassed by this situation, which was creating an unhealthy atmosphere in the class, I confided in a colleague who was a psychologist. He asked me a question that immediately put me on the defensive: "This student seems to present a threat to you," he said. "What nerve in you is she hitting that you're getting upset and so aggressive?" My spontaneous answer was, "She doesn't get to me at all; it's just that she's being ignorant!" But when I reflected on the question and on the vehemence of my reaction, I realized that Agnes was a threat to the "know-it-all-in-me" who claimed to be master of everything in his field and able to answer anything.

For more than a week, I meditated on the "ignorant-in-me"; I talked to it; I asked it how I could make more room for it in my life.

Finally, I walked into class keenly aware of the "ignorant-in-me." When Agnes once again asked me a question that stumped me, I appealed to that repressed side of my personality. I didn't answer the question but asked instead if someone in the class could respond. The second time Agnes interrupted me, the "ignorant-in-me" prompted me to say to her, "Agnes, when someone asks a question, it's often the case that they have already thought about the topic and therefore have the beginnings of an answer. Would you have a rough idea of the answer to your question?" She did not hesitate to offer her reply and I congratulated her.

Following these two interventions by this aspect of my

shadow, the student never again asked me the same frustrating kinds of questions. The climate of animosity between us had disappeared.

The decisive element in the solution was breaking through my resistance to recognizing the "ignorant-in-me," identifying it and letting it take the initiative in my exchanges with Agnes. We both came out of this experience enriched. I recovered the "ignorant-in-me" which I had projected onto her, and she recognized the "intelligent-in-her" which she had projected onto me at the very beginning of the course.

Any psychological wound that is not properly tended to, especially if it was sustained during youth, is liable to nourish the shadow side of our personality.

III. Rediscover your wounded inner child

American author and family therapist John Bradshaw deals with the shadow – although he doesn't use that term – that forms during childhood or adolescence in his book *Homecoming*.[23] After children have been wounded, they relegate to the realms of their unconscious a huge part of themselves. The author explains that any psychological wound that is not properly tended to, especially if it was sustained during youth, is liable to nourish the shadow side of our personality. As soon as we repress an emotion, a character trait, a talent or a way of thinking for fear of disapproval by a teacher or parent, the likely side effect is to cut off our psychic potential. We end up handicapped for the rest of our life.

To begin with, we need to identify in ourselves the wounded part of our inner child which we have tried to hide and forget forever. Once we have discovered in ourselves this child whose wound has not been healed, we need to show great compassion as we choose to "adopt" and look after him or her, for we are dealing with an orphan. The essence of almost all forms of therapy is to become a nourishing parent for ourselves.

It is almost impossible to forgive someone who reflects the negative aspects of our own being unless we first make peace with the unloved parts of ourselves, which we tend to project onto the offender.

The following story recounts the drama of a mother who could no longer tolerate her daughter's attitudes and behaviour. In a letter, she begged me to give her a few tips of some sort to help her correct this adolescent, whom she considered vain, self-centred and full of herself. Then she confided, "I have such an aversion to her that I have real difficulty being reasonable and keeping my self-control in her presence. My daughter will do anything to get attention in both expected and unexpected ways."

Then, a bit later in the letter, she made a truly revealing comment: "My daughter's behaviour reminds me of myself and seems to say to me, 'You were just like her at her age; you wanted to be the centre of attention, but your schemes, far from getting you what you wanted, brought you a lot of disappointment.' I see myself in her so vividly that I am inclined to try to avoid her. In other words, I have the impression I'm rejecting myself when I reject her." She goes on to say that her inability to love her daughter has left her in despair. Finally, she admits that she feels guilty about "being such a bad mother," unable to forgive her daughter for her excesses.

I found this letter very moving because it expressed the anguish of thousands of parents who face the negative side of their shadow projected onto one of their children. Despite her generosity, this woman will have to make peace with herself before she can become a "good mother." For that to happen, she will need to be reconciled to the adolescent in search of love and admiration that she had been, the young woman who had been rebuffed.

Note for the record that it is almost impossible to forgive someone who reflects the negative aspects of our own being unless we first make peace with the unloved parts of ourselves, which we tend to project onto the offender. This is why so many of my readers write to me that, even after reading *How to Forgive: A Step-by-Step Guide*, my book on forgiveness and healing,[24] they have trouble forgiving. I tell them that the first step in the process is to be reconciled to the "inner enemy" which they have projected onto the other person.

In our projections, we must become aware that we are not the object of attacks or humiliations from outside, but that we ourselves seek unconsciously to attack and humiliate others.

IV. Identify with your projections

In *Meeting the Shadow*,[25] an article by Ken Wilber suggests a radical and, at the same time, paradoxical strategy for integrating our shadow. If, for example, we believe, for no objective reason, that we are the target of outside attacks, we have only to reverse the direction of our projection. This will allow us to realize that the hostile emotions or attitudes are coming from us and not from others. In other words, in our projections, we must become aware that we are not the object of attacks or humiliations from outside, but that we ourselves seek unconsciously to attack and humiliate others. The following cases of projection can help us to perform this type of mental gymnastics.

The weak husband who tends to blame his wife and say, "My wife's hostile towards me" would say instead, "I have unexpressed hostile feelings towards my wife and I do everything to make her angry."

The loud and overbearing woman would admit, "I'm afraid to let people see my femininity, which I've always repressed" instead of complaining about "those frail ladies."

The celibate priest, instead of believing he's being seduced by the women he meets, should acknowledge instead, "I'd like to be able to seduce these women, but my official status as a celibate keeps me from doing so."

Instead of being annoyed by his colleague's vulgar

When we recognize that we are responsible for the impulses of our shadow, we can then take ownership of them instead of letting them own us.

manner, the overly-polite professor could well recognize his own fear and say, "I'm afraid of my own inclination to be vulgar, for if I gave in to it, I'd risk scandalizing my family and friends, and being rejected for it."

The workaholic, instead of criticizing those he thinks don't work hard enough, would have to say to himself, "Down deep, I wish I knew how to take time out, but I'm so scared people will think I'm lazy!"

I knew a nun who accused the other nuns of competing with her and trying to outdo her. During our therapy sessions, she became aware of her secret tendency to be competitive and her desire to dominate. Wilber points out that when we recognize that we are responsible for the impulses of our shadow, we can then take ownership of them instead of letting them own us. For this psychic rebalancing to be successful, he recommends that two rules be followed. The first is to "play" your shadow: that is, to identify with it as completely as possible. For example, if I think to myself, "Everybody hates me," I translate this into "I hate everyone." The second recommendation, once you have "played" your shadow, is not to obey the inner feelings or words pushing you to commit nasty deeds. Otherwise you would be like the person who, after having reversed the direction of the projection, said to themselves, "I hate everyone," and started making hateful remarks to people and behaving violently.

Certain people oppose the practice of projection reversal. They fear that in feeling the emotions of the shadow, some people will surrender themselves to it and engage in antisocial and destructive behaviour. At first glance, this objection seems serious. However, it is not as valid as one would think, given the important distinction to be made between feeling and consenting to destructive impulses.

V. Help clients become aware of the two opposing qualities within them

The objective of this strategy is to help a person recognize and welcome two qualities that appear to be contradictory but that in reality complement one another.

The objective of this strategy, which was developed by the well-known American author and hypnotherapist Steve Gilligan, is to help a person recognize and welcome two qualities that appear to be contradictory but that in reality complement one another. The exercise requires the participation of three people: therapist A, therapist B and the client.

Therapist A invites the client to concentrate on themselves. Then she asks them the following question: "Who are you?" The client answers by mentioning one of their qualities, for example, "I am a generous person."

Therapist A then, with great empathy, repeats to them what she has just heard. "I note that you are a generous person"; this is followed by a moment of silence.

Therapist B draws the client's attention to the fact that they also possess the opposite quality: "I also note that you are a person who knows how to take care of yourself." The therapist then says nothing for a moment to allow the client to interiorize the quality that has just been suggested to them. After a moment of silence, both therapists state at the same time in a firm tone, "It's interesting that you can experience these two qualities existing within you simultaneously!" The two therapists then remain silent, allowing the client's Self the time to integrate their last comment.

VI. Harmonize the apparently opposite elements of the ego-ideal (persona) and the shadow

This process, which consists of guiding the projection in the opposite direction, as suggested by Ken Wilber, is currently practised by many well-known therapists.[26] In my view, these

Another means of uncovering the positive aspect of a negative quality or trait is to ask yourself, "What can I learn from such a person?"

techniques produce excellent results in the case of an acute shadow attack (shadowitis). They have proven to be less effective, however, in achieving long-term reintegration.

To help you "embrace" your shadow, I have fine-tuned a strategy whose stages I describe below:

a) Describe a person whom you dislike intensely. Describe clearly the negative quality or trait that you find frightening, annoying or repulsive.

b) Try to discover what positive element this negative quality or trait might hold. In other words, it is a matter of finding the "hidden pearl." Below are some illustrations of this step.

You might discover a person's discretion or diplomacy in an attitude you considered to be "hypocritical."

Upon reflection, we could recognize that a person's tendency to domineer might indicate their desire to take responsibility. That person needs to learn to use that quality without going to extremes.

Another means of uncovering the positive aspect of a negative quality or trait is to ask yourself, "What can I learn from such a person?" If, for example, you detest them for their laziness, you could learn from them how to become more of a "lazy" person yourself, that is to say, to rest, relax, get accustomed to doing less, take little holidays, all of which will help you work better.

c) After you've picked out the positive quality or trait (masked nevertheless by the detestable behaviour of the person towards whom you feel aversion), ask yourself whether you might not need this quality or trait to offset some extreme aspect of your own character. For instance, you are known for your great generosity. You also hate Albert, whom you judge to be selfish. In trying to find the positive flip-side of selfishness, you discover the need to think of yourself more. Thus, to counterbalance your excessive generosity, which would leave you exhausted in the long run, it would be good to think of yourself more often and to know how to say no to certain requests.

The following list provides other examples of persona qualities that are opposite to desired qualities buried in the shadow.

The desirable quality or trait located in the shadow	**The quality or trait of the corresponding persona**
thinking of oneself	generosity
anger	gentleness
introversion	extroversion
being reserved	expressing yourself
openness	discretion
pride in showing one's talents	openness to learning
ability to offer objective criticism	ability to offer encouragement
submissiveness	assertiveness
etc.	etc.

Try this little ritual: using both hands, simulate the coupling of the two qualities or traits and then their reintegration.

Be sure that the qualities or traits of the shadow and the persona really are opposite to one another.

d) Having identified the desirable quality or trait blotted out in the shadow (for example, the ability to take needed rest) as well as the opposite quality or trait belonging to the persona (for example, working yourself to the bone), try this little ritual: using both hands, simulate the coupling of the two qualities or traits and then their reintegration.

Here are the stages to follow for this ritual:

1. Hold your hands about thirty centimetres (12 inches) apart.

2. Imagine you're placing in your dominant hand (the right hand if you are right-handed; the left hand if you are left-handed) a quality or trait that your persona is aware of owning; then, in your other hand, place the desired quality or trait that is buried in your shadow.

3. Dialogue with each of your hands in turn. Acknowledge the quality or trait, accept it and, if necessary, be reconciled to the quality or trait if you have difficulty accepting its existence in you.

4. Be centred within yourself and ask your "integrating" Self to harmonize these two apparently contradictory qualities or traits in such a way that you will see their complementarity.

5. Let your hands move closer together.

6. Stay attentive to the joining of the hands. It symbolizes the reintegration that is taking place between the opposite qualities or traits. Be careful to let the process evolve at its own pace and try not to explain it; it must happen on a subconscious level.

7. Ask the Self to pursue and complete the integration of the two qualities or traits in the days, weeks and months ahead.

8. Finally, gradually leave your state of concentration and become aware of the sounds, colours and smells of your surroundings.

I created a strategy for reintegrating the persona and the shadow based on the first exercise in the work of French psychotherapist M. Berta.

VII. Harmonize the persona and the shadow based on the search for symbols

I created a strategy for reintegrating the persona and the shadow based on the first exercise in the work of French psychotherapist M. Berta.[27] It is designed to be used by a psychotherapist working with a group. Here's what the therapist does:

a) First, I invite the participants to focus clearly on themselves in a relaxed manner.

b) Next, I ask them to let the answers to my questions emerge spontaneously from their imaginations. Then I ask them, "If you were in another world and you could choose another identity, what would you like to become?" Participants have the option of becoming a thing, a plant, an animal or some fictitious character (not a real person).

c) After they've concentrated on this for a few minutes, I ask those who have found the symbol expressing their new identity to raise their hand. If I observe that several participants have not yet found it, I give them more time. Once all have finished, I help the participants emerge from their concentration.

d) Then, each one finds a partner with whom they spend a few minutes describing their symbol. The partner is allowed to ask factual questions such as: Is it big? What colour is it? Does it move? Does it make sounds? Is it far away or nearby? Describe the background of the symbol, its frame of reference. Once the first partner has completed the description, it is the other partner's turn to describe their symbol.

Any mental or rational effort is to remain outside of this work.

e) At the end of this exercise, I invite the participants to go inside themselves again and to answer the following question: "If you were in another world and you could choose another identity, what would you hate to become?" What thing, plant, animal or fictitious character (but not a real person) would you not want to become because you feel such a deep-seated aversion towards this being?

f) After the participants have found their negative symbol, I help them come out of their concentration. They then return to their partner to describe their negative symbol using the same guidelines as in (d). After five minutes, the other partner does the same.

g) After this time for exchange, I ask each participant to choose a quiet spot in the room.

h) Then I ask them to raise their hands to chest level and keep them about thirty centimetres (12 inches) apart. First, for a minute or two, they look at their dominant hand (right, if right-handed; left, if left-handed), in which they imagine they see their positive symbol. Then they look at the opposite hand, in which they imagine they see their negative symbol.

i) I invite them to ask that their Self collaborate in the process of integrating these two symbols. Any mental or rational effort is to remain outside of this work.

j) Then I instruct them to let their hands move closer together in a natural and spontaneous way. I invite them to be open to being surprised by the appearance of a third symbol that the Self will create based on the other two.

If some people feel that something between their hands keeps them from coming together, I suggest that they discover what could be causing this resistance and invite them to eliminate it so they can continue with the exercise.

k) When all have completed the integration of the

positive and the negative symbol, I recommend that they share their discoveries in a group or with their partner. Some like to do a drawing of their third symbol as a reminder of the integration that has taken place.

In these kinds of workshops, I'm always amazed at how frequently the synthesizing symbol takes on a sacred character.

If participants do not successfully complete the reintegration exercise, it is better not to force them.

To counsellors and facilitators: A note of caution regarding the last two strategies. If participants do not successfully complete the reintegration exercise, it is better not to force them. Their unconscious may not be ready to handle this process. It is also possible that because the negative symbol is making too powerful an impact, it is paralyzing the participant. If this is the case, you will need to think of ways to reduce its impact. Changing the size of the symbol might be one strategy. For example, I invited one woman who felt powerless to integrate her negative symbol, a huge boa constrictor, to use her imagination to reduce its size until it was acceptable. Using this technique, she managed to complete the exercise.

VIII. Draw mandalas

The mandala is a symbolic figure composed of a circle and its centre. It appears everywhere in the universe, from the cell, through plant life, to the star nebula. Around the central point is arranged a group of shapes representing various elements. The mandala figure represents both unity and diversity (see page 68 for an example).

This type of figure has often been compared to an eye looking into the psyche. It is found in various religions, particularly because of its unifying function for the person. Indeed, scattered and even opposing elements that lie within

Meditating on and drawing mandalas implicitly involves organizing the disparate elements of our psychic material around the Self.

its circle are attracted to its centre.

The mandala adequately represents the complexity of the psyche: the various parts of the psyche converge on the centre, signifying the Self. The ego, the conscious part, and the shadow, the unconscious part, are situated within the figure's perimeter.

Meditating on and drawing mandalas implicitly involves organizing the disparate elements of our psychic material around the Self. That is why these practices help unify the person and ease the tension caused by a fragmented personality. The whole person then feels that they are on the path of healing and in the process of recovering their inner unity.

To those who wish to explore this path, I recommend the book *Mandalas of the World: A Meditating and Painting Guide.*[28]

THE STORY OF THE SPRING OF LIVING WATER

The living water was tired of flowing underground. One day, it decided to bubble up as a clear and generous spring. People came from far and wide to drink such living, pure, refreshing and healthy water. But alas! A company anxious to make a profit from such a spring bought the property on which it gushed forth, put up securely locked fences and imposed severe restrictions on those who wanted to drink from it. Gradually, only a small, élite group of very well-to-do people were able to go and quench their thirst there. Angry at all the restrictions, the spring decided to bubble up at another spot.

The company continued to sell the water, which had lost its curative, life-giving qualities. However, not many people noticed. Only a few who were dissatisfied with the insipid water being sold to them set out to find the place where the spring of living water had decided to reappear. Happily, they found it.

But soon afterwards, for a second time, the land where the spring appeared was bought up; canals were built and regulations imposed. And once again the spring decided to go underground and show up elsewhere.

Where do you think it moved to?

CHAPTER 8

Reintegration of the Shadow and Spiritual Development

I need to welcome myself unreservedly
and humbly love myself, my whole self,
shadow and light, sweetness and anger,
laughter and tears, humiliation and pride.
I need to reclaim all of my past,
my unadmitted . . . inadmissible . . . past.

– JACQUES LECLERCQ

THE SHADOW AND MORALITY

The shadow is not synonymous with evil

The shadow of the personality is not to be confused with evil. Here is how you can distinguish them from each other. Our shadow was created through the repression of a whole set of feelings, qualities, talents and attitudes that we believed were unacceptable to those around us. Evil, on the other hand, is defined as the privation of a good that is owed: *privatio boni debiti*. Evil does not exist as such; in itself, it is non-being. What does exist is a deficient being or action: that is, one that lacks the perfection it should have. Evil is named in terms of the realities it affects. There will be as many different evils as there are realities affected. In the aesthetic world, it will be the imperfection in a work of art; with respect to health, it will be an illness; in politics, a social upheaval. With respect to morality, evil refers to an action that is not in keeping with its natural purpose; theologically, sin is defined as a break in the relationship of love between a person and God.

It is unfortunate that Jung and his disciples understood the shadow too exclusively in terms of "evil" (the evil part of Self). In so doing, they tended to characterize it as a

The shadow, by virtue of its hidden, primitive and untrained nature, is frightening because it challenges social and ethical rules. However, this does not justify categorizing it as a substantial evil.

substantial evil, an evil that has a real existence. Certainly the shadow, by virtue of its hidden, primitive and untrained nature, is frightening because it challenges social and ethical rules. However, this does not justify categorizing it as a substantial evil. Were it to be considered an evil it could, at the very most, be qualified as structural or organic evil.

If the shadow were a moral evil, we should be fighting it instead of trying to acknowledge and reintegrate it. However, we know only too well that when we decide to battle our shadow, we inevitably fall into its grip and commit precisely the moral errors we wanted to avoid.

William Carl Eichman, a Jungian analyst and author, reminds us that the shadow is part of the human condition and explains why we should convert it, not eliminate it:

> Personal darkness is a type of illness or injury, caused primarily by accidentally cruel programming during childhood, and it should be treated as such. Everyone has a dark nature; it's a condition of life in our world, not a "sin." The goal of the practitioner must be to heal the illness and bring the injured area back into full operation.[29]

A tendency cannot be considered a weakness in itself. On the other hand, the actions that flow freely from it may be qualified as "bad." When ignored and left to itself, the shadow becomes dangerous, for its state of isolation and separateness from the Self may prompt it to act in a diabolical manner (*dia bolè* = separation). On the other hand, if it is acknowledged and integrated, it will co-operate with the integration carried out through the unifying symbols (*sun bolè* = to bring together) of the divine Self.

Acknowledging the drives of your shadow does not mean obeying them

Anyone undertaking serious work on their shadow must not confuse acknowledging and accepting an emotion or impulse as their own with carrying out acts on the prompting of such an emotion or impulse.

To categorize the shadow as a moral evil is an error to which certain intelligent minds are still susceptible. For example, after listening to the tapes of one of my workshops on the shadow, an ethics professor heaped scorn on me. He accused me, among other things, of inciting the workshop participants to follow their basest instincts. He had hardly grasped the distinction that I had clearly established between, on the one hand, acknowledging the existence of and accepting the impulses of our shadow and, on the other, consenting to "carry out the act." It would no doubt have calmed his indignation to remember the classical distinction moralists make between *sentio* and *consentio* (feeling and consenting).

It is important that anyone undertaking serious work on their shadow not confuse acknowledging and accepting an emotion or impulse as their own with carrying out acts on the prompting of such an emotion or impulse. We are not free to feel or not feel an emotion or an impulse: we simply find ourselves experiencing a physiological and psychological fact that imposes its presence. Not acknowledging its existence and not assuming responsibility for it would harm our mental health. Therefore we must, first of all, feel such emotions if we expect to be able to re-appropriate them and recognize that they originate in us. Thus, we will say, "This sexual emotion or this surge of anger belongs to me." Refusing this type of awareness will lead initially to repression, and then to obsessions that will finally be projected onto others. Experienced spiritual directors know this problem well.

A strict moral judgment will therefore be impossible unless the subjects have become aware of the emotions and

In this final chapter, we deal more explicitly with the importance of shadow work from a spiritual point of view.

impulses of their shadow, and have come to own them. Once these conditions are realized, the subjects will be in a position to make free decisions. When they decide to express their feelings, they will need to ask themselves beforehand how they will do so. For example, how do I express anger while still respecting moral criteria? They will try to convey their message without hurting the other person or ruining their relationship with them.

THE SHADOW AND THE SPIRITUAL LIFE

From the start, shadow theory was often implicitly about spirituality. Let us recall here some spiritual aspects of shadow work: The Self is recognized as the spiritual centre of the person; self-knowledge and self-esteem are recognized as essential conditions for spiritual growth; the acknowledgment and acceptance of our shadow depend on the virtue of humility. Doing work on this part of ourselves enables us to adopt a holistic, not a dualistic, perspective on the real; the progressive realization of the Self as the *imago Dei* (image of God) in ourselves counteracts the visions and ambitions of our ego. Note, too, that the theory of the shadow fits well with the words and teachings of Jesus Christ.

In this final chapter, we deal more explicitly with the importance of shadow work from a spiritual point of view. We then describe the times in the spiritual life when this work proves to be necessary. Finally, we will stress the difference between seeking perfection and becoming holy.

Spiritual leaders and their followers need to do their shadow work

It is not so uncommon for someone in a helping profession, whether psychological or spiritual, to lack authenticity because they do not pay attention to the existence of their shadow and their impulses. This neglect has caused some to commit gross moral and professional misdeeds against their clients, followers or students.

Spiritual leaders find that, sooner or later, they are forced to take their shadow into account and to come to terms with it if they wish to advance or help others advance.

The spiritual companion faced with their personal shadow

Many spiritual guides recognize the constant presence and action of the shadow in spiritual growth without using this term. Thus, a great Jesuit preacher was not afraid to refer to "the ungodly element" in himself that he needed to convert. A hospital chaplain recounted that ever since he had become conscious of "the pagan element" in him, he felt more at ease with his non-practising and non-believing patients.

Spiritual leaders find that, sooner or later, they are forced to take their shadow into account and to come to terms with it if they wish to advance or help others advance. In fact, no one travels along a spiritual path as they would along a well-lit and cleared road. Spiritual guides have always had to struggle with their own darkness. Think of Jesus in the desert, of the Buddha, of Mohammed, of all the great saints struggling against temptations, which come in the form of "demons," "Evil," "Satan," "the prince of this world," and so forth.

Even the ordinary praying people can hardly escape this. It doesn't take them long to discover in themselves shadowy regions that they will call their "distractions," their internal conversations, and even their "spiritual nights." Almost all mystics affirm that they have experienced the meanness and trickery of their dark side: pride, hunger for power, jealousy, envy, need for revenge, desire for possession, sexual temptations, and so on. No matter how much zeal you bring to your apostolic action, if you remain unaware of your shadow, you will someday project it onto those to whom you

Katy Butler points out the harmful effects of certain gurus who were not aware of their shadow.

minister and your work will not be fruitful.

A lot of spiritual guides or gurus have ended up exploiting the people they initially claimed to want to help because they have not paid attention to their shadow's intrigues. How many of them, under the pretext of having a spiritual relationship, have more or less consciously established a possessive domination over their "disciples" and used them to satisfy their affective and even sexual needs?

What makes this danger all the greater is that many of those who aspire to the spiritual life are so naïve that they undiscerningly renounce their own judgment in spiritual matters in favour of that of their guide, with the disastrous consequences I have just mentioned. In this regard, we can cite the various scandals that have implicated members of religious orders, ministers of various denominations or founders of sects.

Katy Butler recounts in an article[30] how Buddhist sects were established in California. She points out the harmful effects of certain gurus who were not aware of their shadow, and describes in particular the moral and spiritual degeneration of some of the great Buddhist spiritual leaders who immigrated to the United States. Because of their aura of sanctity, people believed them to be immune to any doctrinal or moral deviation. In fact, many of them succumbed to the temptations of the Western world and used their reputation to legitimate their vices, such as alcoholism, inappropriate sexual behaviour with their followers, an extravagant lifestyle and an unhealthy need to dominate. They brought about their own destruction while doing immense harm to their disciples.

Shadow reintegration work is an essential part of asceticism in spiritual life. The word "asceticism," as used here, is not synonymous with "inhibition."

Others in a helping role

The foregoing reflections are also addressed to any other person in a helping profession or role, be they a psychologist, doctor, social worker or union leader. The weakness that represents a constant pitfall for them is the tendency to project onto their clients their own psychological and spiritual shortcomings. It is easy to predict the outcome: these helpers begin to find it impossible to believe in their clients' psychological and spiritual resources and to respect the path of their progress. They will be inclined to treat them as children, exploit their dependence and even use them to satisfy sexual needs, desire for possession, ambition, and so forth.[31]

Companioning a person on their journey of shadow reintegration

Anyone training others would do well to acquire a sound knowledge of the shadow and its effects on the development of the spiritual life. First of all, such knowledge will make it possible to discern the movements of the Spirit and those of the shadow. It will also enable the guide to lead the trainee through the process of reintegrating his or her untapped resources.

Shadow reintegration work is an essential part of asceticism in spiritual life. The word "asceticism," as used here, is not synonymous with "inhibition." It is wrong, furthermore, to use this word exclusively in the narrow sense of suppression through penance or mortification. Its etymology evokes a much broader meaning, namely that of "exercise," "training" and "practice."

Understood in this way, asceticism consists of reintegrating our shadow rather than repressing it. Too often, spiritual directors simply tell those whom they guide that they must part company with certain weaknesses, but fail to

You can only change within yourself that which you have first effectively accepted.

provide them with a healthy and intelligent way of achieving this. This short-sighted approach only exacerbates the obsessions and compulsions, and locks the person into a vicious circle: sin/failure – confession/admission of guilt – firm resolve not to repeat the action, which then begins all over, and continues indefinitely.

Two cases come to mind where a person's compulsions frustrated the competence of their spiritual director. In the first case, a man who appeared to have a gentle manner subjected those close to him to scenes of uncontrollable anger. For fifteen years this man met with his spiritual director almost every month to get help in mastering his sudden rages. The director would tell him to suppress his fits of anger, go to confession and pray for healing.

The second case deals with a 45-year-old professional man who was incapable of controlling his strong tendency towards ephebophilia (a sexual attraction to adolescents). To satisfy his passion, he would place himself in situations that were dangerous to his physical and moral health as well as to his reputation. At the initial interview, he said he despaired of ever being able to overcome this weakness. He furthermore begged me to forbid him to engage in such deviant behaviour. I then asked him how many spiritual directors or counsellors had forbidden him to continue his sexual activities. At least ten of them had done so. I told him I was not anxious to be the eleventh. However, if he was willing to look at his sexual compulsion, welcome it and seek to transform it, I was prepared to help him.

A fundamental principle in psychotherapy also holds true in spiritual companioning: you can only change within yourself that which you have first effectively accepted. This principle clearly applies to the acceptance and reintegration of your shadow. The two men whose painful situations I have just described did not begin to progress in mastering their compulsions until they had decided to look them in the face, welcome them and befriend them.

In the spiritual life, the novice will likely experience, in turn, states of elation and discouragement.

Meeting the shadow at two decisive stages of the spiritual life

As we saw briefly in the first chapter of this book, there are two periods in our spiritual life when it becomes urgent to pay special attention to the reintegration of the shadow: youth and mid-life. These two periods, which may be called initiatory, mark the beginning of major transitions which require us to effect changes of identity and to create new social ties. Young people must leave behind childhood and adolescence to meet the challenge of taking their place in society. Middle-aged people are led to take stock of their existence, for they can already glimpse the end of their life. Such transformations obviously require us to draw on all our personal resources, especially those of the shadow.

The early stages of the spiritual life

In the spiritual life, the novice will likely experience, in turn, states of elation and discouragement. Sometimes they will have illusions about their degree of perfection, and compare themselves to others with pride, or else with disdain. At other times, they will let themselves get discouraged and witness a re-emergence of bad habits they thought they had mastered.

For this reason they need to be introduced as early as possible to the work of shadow reintegration. With this purpose in mind, their spiritual director or guide will encourage them to confront their inner demons by prescribing a desert experience, where they will live for a

This is the goal of shadow work at the start of the spiritual life: to come face to face with our fears.

period of time a life of deliberately chosen inactivity and solitude. Who are our "demons"? Our obsessions, antipathies, fears and revulsions. Through this asceticism, defined earlier, novices learn to build their spiritual life on a solid psychological foundation, and to digest the various aspects of their shadow. In this way, they will avoid falling prey too frequently to mystical illusions.

Today, we often deplore the absence of initiation practices for young people. In so-called primitive or traditional civilizations, the purpose of the initiatory rite of passage was precisely to allow adolescents to face their fears and separate from their parents so they could enter the adult world. This is the goal of shadow work at the start of the spiritual life: to come face to face with our fears.

A man who aspired to the monastic life woke up one night, paralyzed with fear by the solitude and darkness of his cell. Shaking badly, he got out of bed, barely managed to light a candle and went to knock at the prior's door. The prior received him kindly and listened to him tell of his fright. After reassuring the young monk, he offered to accompany him back to his cell and gestured for him to walk ahead of him along the long, dark corridor. But just as the young man passed in front of him, the prior, with one quick breath, blew out his candle.

The spiritual life in middle age

Because mid-life represents another existential turning point, it also requires us to confront our shadow. It is the point we rightly call the "mid-life crisis." At that age, we have abandoned the naïveté and illusions of youth and have confronted the problem of evil, and death no longer seems something foreign to our own existence. Disappointment in love and failure at various endeavours has taught us more about ourselves. Consequently, we feel less sure about our abilities. We are prone to depression and sometimes even tempted by despair. Doubt has been cast on the old values and assurances, and we have become more susceptible and vulnerable to our "inner demons."

In middle age, it is inevitable that we will meet the part of ourselves that was suppressed by pressure from our surroundings.

At this stage, many are tempted to make a clean break with their previous life: leave their social circle, divorce their partner, change jobs and alter their lifestyle. There is a strong tendency to transfer to others and to circumstances the responsibility for our failures, so we can camouflage our inner unrest. We're tempted to start over from scratch rather than face the inescapable questions: "Who am I?" "What am I going to do with the rest of my life?" These questions cannot be answered satisfactorily unless we approach our shadow.

In middle age, it is inevitable that we will meet the part of ourselves that was suppressed by pressure from our surroundings. So, the man who, until then, has ignored his feminine side will be forced to assume it, while the woman who has hidden her masculine traits will need to be reconciled with them.

The following case illustrates a mid-life crisis well. A priest in his 50s confided to me that while he had always felt so sure of himself before, he found that now he could no longer celebrate Mass in public. From the moment he began putting on his priestly vestments, he felt panic-stricken and would break out in a cold sweat. Just the thought of having to enter the sanctuary made him afraid he was going to faint. A few times he even had to leave the altar to recover from a momentary dizzy spell.

He was upset by what was happening to him. He had always tried to follow a strictly disciplined way of life, to

I encouraged him to listen to this side of himself, which was expressing something deeper than his wish to appear imperturbable and invulnerable.

demonstrate a keen sense of duty and show strength of character. Now he felt weak and depressed. Powerless in the face of the ills afflicting him, he had no choice but to seek help. He was experiencing such turmoil that he considered questioning his vocation. In fact, this priest was failing to recognize the recriminations of his shadow, which was pressuring him to accept his weakness, his emotional life and his dependence.

I helped him understand that what he was really doing was celebrating Mass without having the inner disposition required for this rite. He was re-enacting the mystery of the weak and vulnerable Christ, while displaying the self-assuredness of a sergeant-major in office. As he listened to me, he began to cry uncontrollably, all the while apologizing for doing so. He told me that for the last several years he could not stand to look at the cross without bursting into tears. This spontaneous reaction upset him. I encouraged him to listen to this side of himself, which was expressing something deeper than his wish to appear imperturbable and invulnerable.

During the therapy sessions that followed, this priest gradually learned to acknowledge his sensitive, weak, vulnerable and dependent side. He progressively succeeded in accepting the feminine side of his personality and acquired an awareness of its richness. In his own good time, he began to befriend this other self whose existence he had denied until now. A little later, he confided to me that he had taken up his ministry again. He had resumed celebrating Mass publicly, without any feeling of faintness. He was also sleeping better and no longer needed to take antidepressants. His priestly life was taking a new turn. It was no longer a matter of creating holiness through willpower, but of surrender to the work of grace. He was allowing himself to be touched and led by God's love.

Shadow work is the opposite of seeking moral perfection, if by moral perfection we mean scrupulous conformity to moral rules and to the requirements of our surroundings.

Shadow work and holiness

Perfection and perfectionism

Shadow work is the opposite of seeking moral perfection, if by moral perfection we mean scrupulous conformity to moral rules and to the requirements of our surroundings. This type of perfection is nothing more than *perfectionism,* a perfection that is completely exterior and does not take into account the deep aspirations of the person.

It is often noted that perfectionists limit themselves to exterior criteria which are confused with the ideals of the persona. They will be more anxious to appear as good performers than to seek inner harmony and personal growth.

Consequently, they will often feel anxious and humiliated when they do not manage to live up to the image and the standards of efficiency they have set for themselves. If they happen to make a mistake or experience a reversal of fortune, perfectionists will tend to be self-deprecating and blame themselves relentlessly. In short, they harm themselves in every way. They need to ask themselves whether this violence towards themselves really helps them to grow.

Gandhi is a good example to help us understand how this type of attitude hinders our maturation. Erik Erikson, in his work *Gandhi's Truth,*[32] declares his immense admiration for the pacifist attitude the mahatma maintained throughout the worst conditions of adversity. By his teaching and his example, Gandhi wanted to break the vicious circle of violence. He took blows from his enemies without ever seeking revenge. On the other hand, Erikson did not explain very well how it was that Gandhi, the apostle of non-

Jung considers the unconditional acceptance of self, with its greatness and smallness, to be the heart of the moral question and the highest level of ideal attainable.

violence, could be so violent towards himself on seeing his weaknesses. He loathed himself for not reaching the standards of holiness that he had set for himself. Erikson felt that this attitude was at the root of the lack of tolerance he showed his close family members.

Perfectionists who go to war against their evil inclinations, faults, weaknesses and sins have no chance of making progress morally or spiritually. They nourish their shadow, which they eventually project onto others. People begin to find them abhorrent. Their lack of compassion for themselves and others reinforces their sense of moral failure and their low self-esteem. And so they are caught in a vicious circle of the most debilitating kind. Should we not prefer authentic holiness, which is grace, over the frantic and self-directed search for pseudo-perfection?

Holiness and accepting the unloved parts of ourselves

Jung considers the unconditional acceptance of self, with its greatness and smallness, to be the heart of the moral question and the highest level of ideal attainable.[35] In the same vein, he points out that the practice of charity taught by Jesus Christ should first of all be directed towards ourselves: Whether I feed the hungry, forgive an insult, or love my enemy in the name of Christ, all these acts are a sign of great virtue. "Whatever I do unto the least of these, my brothers and sisters, that I do unto Christ …." But what if I discover that in fact the least of all, the poorest of all the beggars, the most shameless of offenders, my real enemy – all of these live within me, and that I need the help of my own kindness: that I, too, am the enemy who needs to be loved?

Spiritual aspirations even in deviant behaviour

Parts of ourselves, as poor and as deviant as they may be, will show us a store of great riches.

Parts of ourselves, as poor and as deviant as they may be, will show us a store of great riches, on condition that we learn to accept them with intelligence, love and patience.

This statement has been confirmed through Neuro-Linguistic Programming. In this approach, the technique of "Core Transformation" brings astonishing results, for it allows someone to discover spiritual aspirations at the core of the basest compulsions. Here is how it looks. At first, clients are invited to become aware of the presence within them of a "bad" tendency, of an immoral habit or obsession, an entity characteristic of their dark shadow. They are then asked to locate the positive intention that, paradoxically, motivates this compulsion or habit.

Clients are given the time to turn within and question their shadow. They are asked to avoid giving intellectual responses, and to wait instead for an answer to come from their unconscious. Once the answer is found, it is integrated into the earlier question which is then repeated in this new form to motivate the person to go deeper. This process is continued until the client succeeds in discovering the ultimate purpose that their unconscious is pursuing. One of the five following motivations will reveal why a shortcoming or serious fault exists in us: to have a deep sense of inner unity, to be myself, to find lasting peace, to feel acceptable and accepted, to be loved and to love.[36]

Here is a good illustration of the process. I asked an alcoholic person what the positive intention was behind their drinking. The following dialogue ensued:

- It makes me relax.
- And what do you seek in relaxation?
- To feel good and important.

Every so-called bad or compulsive tendency conceals within it a spiritual aspiration towards the good, the beautiful, or the true, towards love or the divine within us.

- What do you gain from feeling good and important?
- A deep desire to finally be myself and to be accepted that way by others.

What can we conclude from the results obtained using the Core Transformation technique? It is evident that every so-called bad or compulsive tendency conceals within it a spiritual aspiration towards the good, the beautiful, or the true, towards love or the divine within us. Applying this technique enables the subject to discover that aspiration and to redirect it. Through my experience with this technique, I have discovered that at the heart of all human filth and scum there always lies a pearl, a treasure. Mixed in with the chaff is the grain. Shadow work consists, then, of extracting this golden nugget from the impurities in which it is embedded.

Holiness and the action of the Self

I have already referred several times to the importance of the action of the Self in the work of reintegrating the shadow. It might be useful at this point to define more clearly the nature and the role of the Self. Through the influence of Carl Jung and his work, psychology has increasingly admitted the existence of a spiritual component to the human being, which Jung calls the Self. According to different spiritual and psychological traditions, it has received various names: "the centre," "the higher self," "the soul," "the deep self," "the organizing principle," "the healing power," and so forth. In any event, in Jung's thinking, the ego (the conscious self) no longer occupies the central place that it had been inclined to take. It now becomes an element in the service of the Self.

Jung was convinced that the Self is "the image of God" in each of us. It contains, then, something divine, making each of us a unique and sacred being of inestimable value. Some claim that when Jung spoke this way, he was affirming the existence of God. He strongly denied this. His affirmation of the existence of the divine Self was the result of scientific observations of human behaviour. And Jung never believed it possible to deduce from scientific observations the metaphysical affirmation of the existence of a Divine Being.

In Carl Jung's view, since the divine Self is common to all humanity, every religious or spiritual tradition describes it.

Psychology needs the support of a sound spirituality

In *Modern Man in Search of a Soul,* Jung writes that, in moments of great distress, human beings spontaneously turn to the great systems of healing, such as those represented by the world religions of Buddhism and Christianity. He goes on to say that all the inventions of human wisdom have never succeeded in healing the most serious psychic illnesses. He writes that we can never succeed in alleviating our suffering through the enlightenment that comes just from our own thinking, but that we must take into account the revelations of a wisdom greater than our own.[37]

In Carl Jung's view, since the divine Self is common to all humanity, every religious or spiritual tradition describes it. While atheists may be alienated by anything evoking the existence, nature or action of God, they too can find something here for them. They will see in the Self an element of the human psyche that they may call, depending on their beliefs, "Love," "my Deep Self," "Wisdom," "my Inner Guide," and so forth.

While the moral and social development of the person is a function of the ego, the work of reconciling the persona and the shadow is carried out by the Self – by virtue of the Self's power to create, heal and organize the whole person. However, this work will only be effective in those who

Holiness is the result of grace or divine action welcomed in complete freedom.

consider the Self a reality that is good, compassionate and filled with love.

What, then, will become of people who have a terrifying idea of the Self? They will never dare to abandon themselves with confidence to its integrative power. In fact, I have met clients who were spiritually incurable because they were haunted by a kind of tyrannical and accusing Superego that they called their "fate" or their "karma." Their spiritual pessimism prevented them from growing. Unless you consider your Self to be a reality filled with tenderness, you will not be able to welcome the dark side of yourself appropriately.

In contrast to a perfection achieved by the efforts of the ego, holiness is the result of grace or divine action welcomed in complete freedom. Here is what Jacques Leclercq writes about this distinction: "Perfection is something I create for myself; holiness is given to me by God. Perfection is at the end of the path I have set for myself; but holiness is given for right now, for the immediate present. Perfection is often humiliated […], holiness never is, […] it is humble."[38]

John Sanford, one of the great Jungian specialists of our time, said in a lecture, "God loves your shadow much more than […] your ego!"[39] He elaborated on his comment, saying, "In a showdown God (Self) favours the shadow over the ego, for the shadow, with all of its dangerousness, is closer to the centre and more genuine."[40]

What happens after shadow reintegration?

At the beginning of this book, I invited you to go on an adventure: that of acknowledging your shadow, meeting it and reintegrating it. Here you are, having reached the end of the undertaking. But it's not over yet! Once you have succeeded in reintegrating part of your shadow, you will move to a new level of consciousness. You will then discover another dark side of yourself that you will need to reintegrate. Work on the shadow is never finished. Each time you welcome part of it, you discover a new landscape of yourself that is waiting to be explored.

Once you have succeeded in reintegrating part of your shadow, you will move to a new level of consciousness.

The work done on your shadow enables you to penetrate further into the spiritual depths of your being. Once you have gone beyond your family, institutional and national shadows, you will need to enter the contrasexual shadow zone, the zone having the traits of the opposite sex. To connect with the richness of the Self (the deep Self), a man will have to welcome his *anima* (his inner woman) with its emotion and sensitivity, while a woman will have to embrace her *animus* (her inner man) with its strength, courage and initiative (see the diagram on the following page).

Jung's concept of the psyche

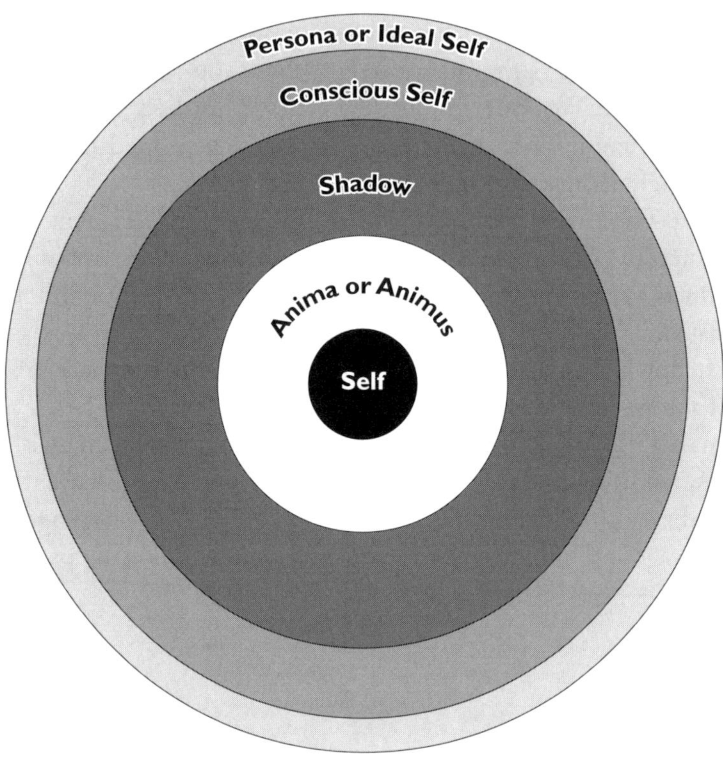

The *Anima* or Inner woman	= The guardians of the Self
The *Animus* or Inner man	

Those who can live their suffering harmoniously will find that when they meet their shadow, they are cleansed of their superficial identities.

Persona, ego, shadow, *anima* or *animus* according to the subject's gender – these are all initiatory stages, milestones on a psychospiritual journey that leads to the heart of the Self. Sometimes we might be tempted to believe that only an intellectual élite is capable of realizing or reaching their *individuation,* to use a Jungian term. Let's not make that mistake. All those who are capable of true asceticism when their shadow emerges will attain communion with their Self. Élite or not, those who can live their suffering harmoniously will find that when they meet their shadow, they are cleansed of their superficial identities. Progressively purified of all artifice, they gradually recognize in themselves their divine nature and discover their calling in the world.

At the close of this book, I would invite you to meditate on the inspiring words of Jacques Grand'Maison, a priest and sociologist, on the benefits of reintegrating the shadow:

> Encounters with the shadow will mine a depth of soul, unearth a memory, open up a horizon … but, above all, they will lead us to an inner wellspring that can revive our passion for life, our desire to love, our will to struggle and the courage to move boldly forth into the future.[41]

NOTES

1 Liliane Frey-Rohn, in C. Zweig and J. Abrams, eds. *Meeting the Shadow: The Hidden Power of the Dark Side of Human Nature,* Los Angeles, Jeremy P. Tarcher, 1991, p. xvii.
2 See C.G. Jung, *Psychology and Religion: West and East* (Collected Works, 7), Bollingen Series, Princeton: Princeton University Press, 1938, p.528.
3 S. Naifeh, "Archetypal Foundations of Addiction and Recovery," in *Journal of Analytical Psychology,* 40 (1995), p. 148.
4 G. Egan, *Working the Shadow Side: A Guide to Positive Behind-the-Scenes Management,* San Francisco, Jossey-Bass, 1994.
5 M. Bowles, "The Organization Shadow," in *Organization Studies,* 12 (3), 1991, pp. 387-404.
6 See C.G. Jung, *Psychology and Religion: West and East* (Collected Works, 7), Bollingen Series, Princeton University Press, 1938, p. 140.
7 C.G. Jung, *Aion* (Collected Works, 9, Part II), Bollingen Series, Princeton University Press, 1951, p. 14.
8 J. Grand'Maison, L. Baroni, J. Gauthier, *Les défis des générations: enjeux sociaux et religieux du Québec d'aujourd'hui* [The challenges of the generations: the social and religious stakes in Quebec today] (Cahiers d'études pastorales 15), Saint-Laurent, Quebec, Fides, 1995, p. 360.
9 C.G. Jung, *Memories, Dreams, Reflections,* New York, Pantheon Books, 1963, pp. 87-88.
10 Cited in C. Zweig, *op.cit.,* p. 3.
11 D. M. Dooling, "The Wisdom of the Contrary," in *Parabola, the Trickster,* vol. 5, no. 1 (1979), p. 55.
12 D.W. Winnicott, *Maturation Processes and the Facilitating Environment: Studies in the Theory of Emotional Development,* New York: International Universities Press, 1965, p. 140. [Winnicott is an English psychologist specializing in child psychology.]
13 E. Berne, *Games People Play: The Basic Handbook of Transactional Analysis,* New York, Grove Press, 1964.

14 Zweig, *op.cit.*, p. 265.

15 R. Coté, "Dieu chante dans la nuit: l'ambiguïté comme invitation à croire"(God sings in the night: ambiguity as an invitation to believe) in *Concilium* 242 (1992), p. 120.

16 Zweig, *op. cit.*, p. 32.

17 R.A. Johnson, *Owning Your Own Shadow: Understanding the Dark Side of the Psyche*, San Francisco, Harper, 1991. Johnson, a Jungian analyst, is a renowned speaker. He has also written numerous books, including *He: Understanding Masculine Psychology, She: Understanding Feminine Psychology, We: Understanding the Psychology of Romantic Love.*

18 Johnson, *op. cit.*, pp. 85-90.

19 Cited in Zweig, *op. cit.*, p. xix.

20 K. Wilber, *The Spectrum of Consciousness,* Wheaton, IL, Theosophical Publishing House, 1982, p. 203.

21 M.-L. von Franz, *Projection and Re-Collection in Jungian Psychology: Reflections of the Soul,* La Salle, Illinois, Open Court, 1980, p. 3.

22 M.-L. von Franz, *op. cit.*, p. 25.

23 J. Bradshaw, *Homecoming: Reclaiming and Championing Your Inner Child,* New York, Bantam, 1990.

24 J. Monbourquette, *How to Forgive: A Step-by-Step Guide,* Ottawa/ Cincinnati/London, Novalis/St. Anthony Messenger Press/Darton, Longman and Todd, 2000.

25 Zweig, *op. cit.*, pp. 275-276.

26 Professionals will recognize this strategy among the following therapists: Fritz Perls and his "reverse polarity game with the empty chair," Milton Erickson and the "utilization of resistance," Paul Watzlawick and "prescribing the symptom" and Viktor Frankl and the "practice of paradoxical intention."

27 M. Berta, *Prospective symbolique en psychothérapie. L'épreuve d'anticipation clinique at expérimentale* (symbolic prospective in psychotherapy. clinical and experimental anticipation test), Paris, Editions ESF, 1983.

28 R. Dahlke, *Mandalas of the World: A Meditating and Painting Guide.* New York, Sterling Publishing Co., 1992.

29 Zweig, *op. cit.*, p. 136.

30 "Encountering the Shadow in Buddhist America," in Zweig, *op. cit.*, pp. 137-147.

31 Readers who are interested in pursuing this subject further would benefit from reading *Power in the Helping Professions* (Dallas, Spring Publications, 1971), a work by Adolf Guggenbühl-Craig, a priest and Jungian psychoanalyst.

32 E. Erikson, *Gandhi's Truth: On the Origins of Militant Nonviolence,* 1st ed., New York, Norton, 1969. (Erik Erikson is a psychologist and specialist in human development.)

33 See C.G. Jung, *Psychology and Religion: West and East* (Collected Works, 7), Bollingen Series, Princeton University Press, 1938, p. 241.

34 A new approach to learning developed in the United States in the early 70's by Richard Bandler and John Grinder.

35 C. Andreas, *Core Transformation: Reaching the Wellspring Within,* Moab, Utah, Real People Press, 1994.

36 Ibid., p. 19.

37 See C.G. Jung, *Modern Man in Search of a Soul,* New York, A Harvest Book, 1969, pp. 240-241.

38 *Vie chrétienne* (Christian life), March 1983.

39 John Sanford, quoted by Robert Johnson in *Owning Your Own Shadow: Understanding the Dark Side of the Psyche,* San Francisco, Harper, 1991, p. 44.

40 Ibid., p. 45.

41 Grand'Maison, *op. cit.*, p. 372.

BIBLIOGRAPHY

Andreas, C. *Core Transformation: Reaching the Wellspring Within.* Moab, Utah: Real People Press, 1994.

Bly, R. *A Little Book on the Human Shadow.* San Francisco: Harper and Row, 1988.

Bowles, M. *"The Organization Shadow."* Organization Studies, 1991, 12, (3), pp. 387-404.

Bradshaw, *J. Homecoming: Reclaiming and Championing Your Inner Child.* New York: Bantam, 1992.

Brewi, J. and A. Brennan. *Celebrate Mid-Life: Jungian Archetypes and Mid-Life Spirituality.* New York: Crossroad, 1988.

Côté, R. "Dieu chante dans la nuit: l'ambiguïté comme invitation à croire." *Concilium,* 1992, 242, pp. 117-128.

Dahlke, R. *Mandalas of the World: A Meditating and Painting Guide.* New York: Sterling Publishing Co., 1992.

Dooling, D.M. "The Wisdom of the Contrary." *Parabola, the Trickster,* 1979, vol. 5, no. 1, pp. 54-65.

Egan, G. *Working the Shadow Side: A Guide to Positive Behind-the-Scenes Management.* San Francisco: Jossey-Bass, 1994.

Franz, M.-L. von. *Projection and Re-Collection in Jungian Psychology: Reflections of the Soul.* La Salle, Illinois: Open Court, 1980.

Franz, M.-L. von. *Shadow and Evil in Fairy Tales.* Zurich: Spring Publications, 1974.

Grand'Maison, J., L. Baroni, J. Gauthier. *Les défis des générations: enjeux sociaux et religieux du Québec d'aujourd'hui* (Cahiers d'études pastorales 15). Saint-Laurent, Quebec: Fides, 1995.

Green, Julien. *L'homme et son ombre.* Paris: Seuil, 1991.

Guggenbühl-Craig, A. *Power in the Helping Professions.* Dallas: Spring Publications, 1971.

Hopcke, R.H. *Persona: Where Sacred Meets Profane.* Boston: Shambhala Publications, 1995.

Idel, M. *Golem: Jewish Magical and Mystical Traditions on the Artificial Anthropoid.* Albany, NY: State University of New York Press, 1990.

Johnson, R.A. *Owning Your Own Shadow: Understanding the Dark Side of the Psyche.* San Francisco: Harper, 1991.

Jung, C.G. *Aion* (Collected Work, 9, Part II), Bollingen Series. Princeton: Princeton University Press, 1951.

Jung, C.G. et al. *Man and His Symbols.* New York: Dell Publishing, 1968.

Jung, C.G. *Memories, Dreams, Reflections.* New York: Pantheon Books, 1963.

Jung, C.G. *Modern Man in Search of a Soul.* New York: A Harvest Book, 1969.

Jung, C.G. *Psychology and Religion: West and East* (Collected Works, 7), Bollingen Series. Princeton: Princeton University Press, 1938.

Kopp, S. *Mirror, Mask and Shadow: The Risk and Rewards of Self-Acceptance.* New York: Bantam, 1982.

Mattoon, M.A. (Ed.) *The Archetype of Shadow in a Split World.* Tenth International Congress for Analytical Psychology (Berlin, September 1986). Zurich: Daimon Verlag, 1987.

Miller, W.A. *Make Friends with Your Shadow: How to Accept and Use Positively the Negative Side of Your Personality.* Minneapolis: Augsburg, 1981.

Miller, W.A. *Your Golden Shadow: Discovering and Fulfilling Your Undeveloped Self.* San Francisco: Harper & Row, 1989.

Moore, R.L. (Ed.) *Carl Jung and Christian Spirituality.* New York: Paulist Press, 1988.

Moseley, Douglas & Naomi. *Dancing in the Dark: The Shadow Side of Intimate Relationships.* Georgetown, MA: North Star Publications, 1994.

Naifeh, S. "Archetypal Foundations of Addiction and Recovery." *Journal of Analytical Psychology*, 1995, 40, pp. 133-159.

Neumann, E. *Depth Psychology and a New Ethic.* New York: Harper, 1969.

Perera, S.B. *The Scapegoat Complex: Towards a Mythology of Shadow and Guilt.* Toronto: Inner City Books, 1986.

Richo, D. *Shadow Dance: Liberating the Power and Creativity of Your Dark Side.* Boston: Shambhala, 1999.

Sanford, J.A. *Evil: The Shadow Side of Reality.* New York: Crossroad, 1981.

Sanford, J.A. *The Strange Trial of Mr. Hyde: A New Look at the Nature of Human Evil.* San Francisco: Harper & Row, 1987.

Sweeney, R. *You and Your Shadow* (audio recording). Cincinnati: St. Anthony Messenger Press, 1988.

Vieljeux, J. "La persona." *Cahiers jungiens de psychoanalyse,* 1988, 58, 3rd trimester, pp. 3-18.

Whitmont, E.C. *The Symbolic Quest.* Princeton: Princeton University Press, 1991.

Wilber, K. *The Spectrum of Consciousness.* Wheaton, IL: Theosophical Publishing House, 1982.

Winnicott, D.W. *Maturation Processes and the Facilitating Environment: Studies in the Theory of Emotional Development.* New York: International Universities Press, 1965.

Wolff-Salin, M. *The Shadow Side of Community and the Growth of the Self.* New York: Crossroad, 1988.

Zweig, C. and J. Abrams (Eds.) *Meeting the Shadow: The Hidden Power of the Dark Side of Human Nature.* Los Angeles: Jeremy P. Tarcher, 1991.

Zweig, C. and S. Wolf. *Romancing the Shadow.* New York: Ballantine Wellspring, 1997.

ALSO BY JOHN MONBOURQUETTE

How to Forgive
A Step-by-Step Guide

"What does it take to forgive?" asks John Monbourquette, best-selling author, psychologist and priest. His answer is a unique twelve-step guide which offers profound and practical advice on overcoming the emotional, spiritual and psychological blocks to true forgiveness.

Monbourquette begins by exploring the nature of forgiveness and exploding some of the myths. He shows how essential forgiveness is for us all, whatever our beliefs, for forgiveness touches on all aspects of the human person, the biological and psychological as well as the spiritual. He then takes the reader through his twelve-step healing process, providing practical exercises, case histories, anecdotes and even poetry along the way.

How to Forgive is an honest and touching book which unlocks the liberating and transformative power of forgiveness.

- 198 pages
- paperback

Quebec, Canada
2001